Herbert Spencer, Fred Newton Scott, T. H Wright

The Philosophy of Style

Together with an Essay on style. Second Edition

Herbert Spencer, Fred Newton Scott, T. H Wright

The Philosophy of Style
Together with an Essay on style. Second Edition

ISBN/EAN: 9783337079239

Printed in Europe, USA, Canada, Australia, Japan

Cover: Foto ©Thomas Meinert / pixelio.de

More available books at **www.hansebooks.com**

The Academy Classics

HERBERT SPENCER

PHILOSOPHY OF STYLE

TOGETHER WITH

AN ESSAY ON STYLE

By T. H. WRIGHT

WITH INTRODUCTION AND NOTES

BY

FRED N. SCOTT, Ph.D.

PROFESSOR OF RHETORIC IN THE UNIVERSITY OF MICHIGAN

SECOND EDITION

1917

ALLYN AND BACON

Boston   New York   Chicago

Typography by J. S. Cushing & Co., Boston.

Presswork by Berwick & Smith, Boston.

PREFACE.

THIS volume may be considered as the second of a series,— Lewes's 'Principles of Success in Literature' being the first,— the object of which is to bring helpful discussions of the principles of literary criticism within the reach of teachers of rhetoric. As before, the plan has been followed of providing a biographical and critical introduction, an index, and a few notes,— the latter designed to provoke discussion or to furnish clues for further investigation, rather than to exhibit in their totality the results of the editor's researches.

To Spencer's essay, which makes up the bulk of the pamphlet, has been added, as a commentary upon 'The Philosophy of Style,' a paper by T. H. Wright, originally published in *Macmillan's Magazine*, Vol. XXXVII., p. 78, and afterwards reprinted in the *Popular Science Monthly*, Vol. XII., p. 340. In the appendices will be found a note from Gurney's 'Power of Sound,' criticising Spencer's theory of the effect of rhythmical structure, and a long extract from Spencer's 'First Principles,' touching the evolution of literature. These will prove helpful where the originals cannot be readily consulted.

In the belief that 'The Philosophy of Style' can be understood only in its proper connection with the Spencerian philosophy as a whole, the Introduction has been made largely bibliographical. The references to Spencer's articles in magazines will in some cases supply the lack of books. Articles upon Spencer's life and personality are not very numerous. The best biographical sketch is that in the *Popular Science Monthly*, Vol. VIII., p. 620. Briefer accounts will be found in 'Men of the Time,' Brockhaus' 'Conversations-Lexikon,' and the recent article by Mr. W. H. Hudson, in the *Arena* for February, 1892. Discussions and criticisms of Spencer's philosophical views, are, on the other hand, exceedingly numerous. A favorable estimate, giving a brief summary of Spencer's more important writings down to 1874, is available in the article by E. L. Youmans, entitled 'Herbert Spencer and the Doctrine of Evolution,' *Popular Science Monthly*, Vol. VI., p. 20. A careful outline of the Spencerian philosophy, from a decidedly different point of view, is given by Dr. W. T. Harris in the *Journal of Speculative Philosophy*, Vol. I., p. 6. T. H. Green's criticisms in the *Contemporary Magazine*, Vol. XXXI., pp. 25 and 745, Vol. XXXII., p. 82, are well known. The best induction to the subject, barring the original works, is, of course, John Fiske's 'Cosmic Philosophy.'

FRED N. SCOTT.

Ann Arbor, February 9, 1892.

PREFACE TO THE SECOND EDITION.

A second edition gives opportunity for correcting a few typographical errors, and for inserting a few references that have recently come to my attention. I take advantage of this preface to add to the list of critical works and essays the recent volume by Professor W. H. Hudson, 'Introduction to the Philosophy of Herbert Spencer' (N. Y.: 1894).

FRED N. SCOTT.

CONTENTS.

———◄◦►———

SPENCER'S PHILOSOPHY OF STYLE.

PART I. — CAUSES OF FORCE IN LANGUAGE WHICH DEPEND UPON ECONOMY OF THE MENTAL ENERGIES.

PART II. — CAUSES OF FORCE IN LANGUAGE WHICH DEPEND UPON ECONOMY OF THE MENTAL SENSIBILITIES.

WRIGHT'S ESSAY ON STYLE.

INTRODUCTION.

———∘०%⊛%००———

LIFE AND WRITINGS.

HERBERT SPENCER's life may be divided into three
periods: his boyhood and schooling, his experience as a
practical engineer, the years that he has spent in develop-
ing his system of philosophy. The first period comprises
seventeen years. He was born in Derby, England, April
27, 1820. His father was a school-teacher, a man of considerable learning and much force of character, a liberal in
both politics and religion, in matters of education inclined
to throw emphasis upon the value of observation and the
study of the sciences. From such a father, and later from
an uncle who held similar views, Herbert's early education,
in so far as he got it from others, was mainly received.
Reputed inattentive, idle, and disobedient, he was by no
means a model scholar. In fact he did not learn to read
until seven years of age. It is noteworthy, however, that
he rebelled only against learning by rote; for tasks requir-
ing originality and independent investigation his mind
showed itself unusually capable. During these early years
he studied drawing and mechanics, made collections of
insects, read a little ancient history, and absorbed a good
deal of science and politics from the conversations of his
father's friends at meetings of the Derby Philosophical
Society. From 1833 to 1836 he was with his uncle, the Rev.
Thomas Spencer of Hinton, nominally preparing for one
of the universities, but in reality neglecting Greek and
Latin for mathematics and mechanics. At his own wish,

the idea of a university career, which his uncle had entertained for him, was abandoned. He returned home, spent a year in study, and seven months, not unsuccessfully, in teaching. To this period belongs his first literary work — a discussion of a geometrical theorem published in the *Civil Engineer's and Architect's Journal.*

The second portion of Spencer's life begins with an invitation, given him in the fall of 1837, to go to London as a railroad surveyor and draughtsman. For the following ten years his time was divided between practical work — testing machinery, designing, and constructing — and miscellaneous reading and study. While secretary to the chief engineer of the Birmingham and Gloucester Railroad he devised a velocimeter for recording the speed of locomotives. In 1841, refusing a proffered engagement as engineer, he returned home to spend two years in scientific studies. An overflow of the river at Derby led to his preparing for the town council a detailed report upon the causes of the overflow, with proposals for a remedy. A second visit to London was undertaken with a view to securing a position with some literary or scientific journal, but an engineering job was taken up instead. A third visit was made in 1844 with like results. Then came a depression in railroad enterprises and a consequent falling-off in the demand for young engineers. In 1846 Spencer returned home, and although some time for the next two years was devoted to invention and problems in mechanics, engineering as a profession was, in 1848, definitely abandoned. During these ten years Spencer's studies had laid the foundation for the development of his philosophical system. Among other scientific works he had taken up Lyell's 'Principles of Geology,' and after reading the author's attack upon what was then known as Lamarck's 'Development-theory,' had ranged himself upon the side of the French naturalist. From this year, 1839, may be dated the beginning of Spencer's prolonged effort to interpret all the facts of nature in the light of the central principle, evolution. Other studies occupying his leisure hours were drawing, botany, social science, and, for a brief space, phrenology. His writings during this period embrace technical articles in the *Civil Engineer's Journal;* a series of letters, published in the *Nonconformist* in 1842, on 'The Proper Sphere of Government,' tending to show that the government's sole function should be the protection of life, of property-tenure, and of social order; and miscellaneous contributions to the *Philosophical Magazine* and the *Zoöist.*

A third period may be said to begin either in 1846 when he conceived, or in 1848 when he began writing, what is properly the earliest of his philosophical works — the 'Social Statics.' Published in 1850, this work is an attempt to account for the social organism as a growing adaptation of men to their environment. Together with the 'Theory of Population,' published in the *Westminster Review* in 1832, and 'The Development Hypothesis' which appeared in the *Leader* the same year, it forms a remarkable anticipation of the theory which Darwin put forth nine years later. From 1848 to 1852 Spencer was connected as editorial writer with the *Economist,* a London journal. The essay on 'The Philosophy of Style' came out in the *Westminster Review* for October of the latter year. In the same magazine appeared, the following year, articles on 'Over-Legislation,' upholding the theory first broached in the *Nonconformist;* and 'The Universal Postulate,' an examination of Mill. Three essays came from Spencer's pen in 1854: 'The Genesis of Science,' *British Quarterly Review* for July, in which Comte's classification of the sciences is attacked; 'The Art of Education,' *North British Review* for May; and 'Manners and Fashion,' *Westminster* for April. In August he began his 'Principles of Psychology.' The next year saw the completion of this book, but over-work brought on a nervous break-down, which left the author a semi-invalid for the rest of his life. Nevertheless the stream of his incessant activity was barely interrupted. Four articles by him are to be found in the reviews for 1857. In 'Progress, its Law and Cause,' in the *Westminster Review*, the idea of evolution in its broad application to all physical, biological, and social phenomena, which had first come to him while writing the 'Principles of Psychology,' was set forth at considerable length. 'The Origin and Function of Music,' appearing in *Fraser's Magazine* for October, aimed to explain the nature of musical expression as an idealization of the cadences of emotional speech. Other essays were 'Representative Government, What is it good for?' *Westminster* for October, and 'Transcendental Physiology,' *National Review* for October. During the next three years magazine articles appeared at intervals of a few months. 'State Tamperings with Money and Banks' came out in January, 1858, 'Moral Education' in the *British Quarterly Review* for April, 'The Nebular Hypothesis,' a defence of the theory, in the *Westminster* for July, and a review of Professor Owen's 'Archetype and Homologies of the Vertebrate Skeleton' in the *Medico-chirurgical Review* for October. For 1859 may be found, 'The Laws of Organic Form' in the *Medico-chirurgical Review* for January, 'Physical Education,' a continuation of 'Moral Education,' in the *British Quarterly* for April, 'Morals of Trade' in *Westminster* for April, 'What Knowledge is of Most Worth?' in the *Westminster* for July, and 'Illogical Geology' in the *Universal Review* of the same month. Two articles appeared in January of the following year. 'Social Organism,' in the *Westminster*, was an attempt to discover in the growth of society the same principle which is seen to determine the growth of the individual organism. The other essay was a review of Bain's 'The Emotions and the Will.' To the same year belong 'The Physiology of Laughter,' *Macmillan's Maga-*

zine, 'Parliamentary Reforms, their Dangers and Safe-
guards,' *Westminster Review,* and 'Prison Ethics,' *British
Quarterly Review* for July.

It was not until 1858, while writing the article on the 'Nebular Hypothesis,' that Spencer came to understand toward
what goal his mental activity was tending. At that time
there occurred to him the idea of a system of philosophy in
which evolution should figure as the central co-ordinating
principle for the interpretation of all the sciences. The development of this system he resolved to make the task of his
remaining years. In order to get the necessary means and
leisure, since his books thus far published had been a source
of expense rather than of income, he at first applied for a
position under government, but meeting with no success in
that direction, determined to publish the work on subscrip-
tion. Accordingly a prospectus of the 'System of Philosophy,' to comprise treatises on Biology, Psychology, Sociology,
and Ethics, was issued in March, 1860, and the first install-
ment of the series sent out in October. The initial volume,
entitled 'First Principles,' was completed, June, 1862. From
that time to the present most of Spencer's strength has been
given to the filling-in of the outline furnished by his prospectus. The 'Principles of Biology' appeared in 1867, a
corrected and enlarged edition of the 'Principles of Psychology' in 1872. For the 'Principles of Sociology' an
immense number of data was collected through the aid of
readers at the universities, and published in tabular form
in a series of eight quartos, entitled 'Descriptive Sociology.'
These volumes began appearing in 1873, accompanied by a
preliminary work on the 'Study of Sociology.' Of the main
work, the first part appeared in 1874, the remaining volumes, 'Ceremonial Institutions,' 'Political Institutions,'
and 'Ecclesiastic Institutions,' coming out at intervals
during the next ten years. Parts VII. and VIII. of Vol. 2,
on 'Professional Institutions, and 'Industrial Institutions,'

and the whole of Vol. 3, on 'Social Progress,' are yet unwritten. In the third main department of his system, 'The Principles of Morality,' but two volumes have been issued, the 'Data of Ethics' (1879), and 'Justice,' which last is published the current year.

While actively engaged upon this great work, Spencer has continued his contributions to the periodicals. In 1864–5 he published in the *Reader*, articles on 'What is Electricity?' 'Constitution of the Sun,' 'Political Fetichism,' and 'The Collective Wisdom.' The first volume of the *Fortnightly* (1865) contained an article by him on 'Mill *vs.* Hamilton.' In 1867 he contributed an essay 'On Political Education' to E. L. Youman's 'Culture Demanded by Modern Life.' 'Spontaneous Generation and the Hypothesis of Physiological Units' appeared in the first volume of *Appleton's Magazine* (1869), and was republished in book form the following year. In the *Fortnightly* for May, 1870, and December, 1871, are articles on 'The Origin of Animal Worship' and 'Specialized Administration.' Other essays in English periodicals are 'Mr. Martineau on Evolution,' *Contemporary Review* for April, 1872, 'Replies to Criticisms' in the *Fortnightly* for November and December, 1873, 'Factors of Organic Evolution,' *Nineteenth Century* for April and May, 1886, 'Origin of Music,' *Mind* for October, 1890. In this country the *Popular Science Monthly* has been active in reprinting Spencer's articles from the English magazines, as well as in publishing original contributions from him. Among these papers are the following: 'Punishing a Senior Wrangler' (Vol. 5, p. 144), 'Consciousness under Chloroform' (13:694), 'The Coming Slavery' (24:721), 'The New Toryism' (24:433), 'The Great Political Superstition' (25:289), 'Retrogressive Religion' (25:451), 'Origin of the Synthetic Philosophy' (26:30), 'Last Words about Agnosticism' (25:310), 'A Rejoinder to M. de Laveleye' (27:188), 'A Counter Criticism' (33:150), 'The Ethics of

Kant' (33:464), 'Absolute Political Ethics' (36:608), 'Letters on the Land Question' (36:334, 507). Most of Spencer's writing for the magazines has been republished in book form, either as integral portions of the 'Synthetic Philosophy,' or as volumes of miscellaneous essays. Among the latter are 'Illustrations of Universal Progress,' 'Essays, Moral, Political, and Æsthetic,' 'Recent Discussions in Science, Philosophy, and Morals,' and 'The Man *vs.* the State.' The following essays, not previously mentioned, are to be found in these collections:—'Use and Beauty,' 'Gracefulness,' 'Sources of Architectural Types,' 'Personal Beauty,' 'Use of Anthropomorphism.' In the 'Recent Discussions' have been incorporated two essays, 'The Classification of the Sciences' and 'Reasons for Dissenting from the Philosophy of Comte,' which first appeared in book form in 1864.

Besides the appearance of these books and essays, but two events have marked the later years of a life outwardly, at least, most uneventful. One was Mr. Spencer's brief visit to the United States in 1882, when, unfortunately, the state of his health debarred him from personal contact with representative men and institutions; the other his election to the French Academy in 1883, as corresponding member in place of Emerson. This third period of his life has thus been pre-eminently that of the scholar and writer. It is not improbable that, under other physical conditions, he might have sought outlet for his practical nature in public life or in experimental science. But the necessity of husbanding his energies has forbidden arduous labor of either kind. Able to endure, from the age of thirty-five, barely three working hours a day, Mr. Spencer has been compelled all the latter portion of his life, in science to act as interpreter of other men's discoveries, in politics to content himself with those tardy changes in legislation which have come from the slow assimilation of his ideas by the public mind.

Mr. Spencer's contribution to the history of thought, while probably smaller than many of his followers have claimed, is undoubtedly very great. First, and most important of all, he brought home to the British mind, by the announcement of his plan of work, a conception of the necessity and value of philosophic interpretation. He virtually asserted, in his prospectus, that all knowledge is one, that the same essential principle underlies all phenomena. This was to be expected from a "Germanizing transcendentalist," and from such a thinker would have been looked upon as so much theorizing; but coming from a hard-headed scientist, an engineer and student of biology, it could not fail to produce a profound impression. To Spencer, therefore, must be credited, in very large part, the awakening of the philosophic spirit in both England and America.

In the second place, to Spencer more perhaps than to any other Englishman are due the development, the application, and the popularizing of the theory of evolution. In his essay on 'Reasons for Dissenting from the Philosophy of Comte' he states for himself the part this idea has played in the formulation of his philosophical belief:

"And now let me point out that which really has exercised a profound influence over my course of thought. The truth which Harvey's embryological inquiries first dimly indicated, which was afterward more clearly perceived by Wolff, and which was put into a definite shape by Von Baer — the truth that all organic development is a change from a state of homogeneity to a state of heterogeneity — this it is from which very many of the conclusions which I now hold have indirectly resulted. In 'Social Statics' there is everywhere manifested a dominant belief in the evolution of man and of society. There is also manifested the belief that this evolution is in both cases determined by the incidence of conditions — the actions of circumstances. And there is, further, in the section above referred to, a recognition of the fact that organic and social evolutions conform to the same law. Falling amid beliefs in evolutions of various orders, everywhere determined by natural causes (beliefs again displayed in the 'Theory of Population' and in the 'Principles of Psychology'), the formula of Von Baer acted as an organizing principle. The extension of it to other kinds of phenomena than those of individual and social organization is traceable through successive stages. It may be seen in the last paragraph of an essay on 'The Philosophy of Style,' published in October, 1852; again in an essay on 'Manners and Fashion,' published in April, 1854; and then in a comparatively advanced form in an essay on 'Progress: its Law and Cause,' published in April, 1857. Afterward there came the recognition of the need for further limitation of this formula; next the inquiry into those general laws of force from which this universal trans- formation necessarily results; next the deduction of these from the ultimate law of the persistence of force; next the perception that there is everywhere a process of Dissolution complementary to that of Evolution; and finally, the deter- mination of the conditions (specified in the foregoing essay) under which Evolution and Dissolution respectively occur."

'THE PHILOSOPHY OF STYLE.'

In the 'Prospectus' distributed in 1860 is announced 'The Principles of Sociology' in three volumes. The third vol- ume, containing Parts VII.–XI., was to embrace the follow- ing subjects: — Part VII., Lingual Progress, "the evolution of Languages regarded as a psychological progress deter- mined by social conditions"; Part VIII., Intellectual Prog- ress, "treated from the same point of view: including the growth of classifications; the evolution of science out of common knowledge; the advance from qualitative to quantitative prevision, from the indefinite to the definite, and from the concrete to the abstract"; Part IX., Æsthetic Progress, "the Fine Arts similarly dealt with: tracing their gradual differentiation from primitive institutions and from each other, their increasing varieties of development, and their advance in reality of expression and superiority of aim"; Part X., Moral Progress, "exhibiting the genesis of the slow emotional modifications which human nature undergoes in its adaptation to the social state"; Part XI., The Consensus, "treating of the necessary interdependence of structures and of functions in each type of society, and in the successive phases of social development." Concerning Part IX. a footnote says, "Two papers on 'The Origin and Function of Music' and 'The Philosophy of Style' contain some ideas to be embodied in Part IX."[1] From these data we may infer that the paper on 'The Philosophy of Style' was regarded by Spencer as a fragment of a treatise on Sociology, and that in it literature is dealt with as one of the fine arts, being considered a psychological phenomenon determined by social conditions. It must be remembered, however, that at the time the essay was written, the main outlines of the system were as yet somewhat vague. The author himself did not fully appreciate the trend of his own utterances. Consequently in his treatment of Style he does not make much use of that conception of the social organism which in the completed work was to have played so important a part. The essay remains a fragment, not to be rightly understood until it is inserted in the place which the author intended it should occupy. This is a task which, let us hope, Mr. Spencer may be spared to accomplish; meanwhile it may be

---

[1] To these should be added the papers that appeared later on 'Gracefulness,' 'Use and Beauty,' 'The Sources of Architectural Types,' 'Personal Beauty' and the recent essay on 'The Origin of Music' (*Mind*, 1890).

permitted the present writer to indicate, very briefly, the line of treatment which seems to him to be demanded by the nature of the subject.

'THE PRINCIPLE OF ECONOMY.'

In the opening chapter of the 'Data of Ethics' the author writes:

"If the part is conceived without any reference to the whole, it becomes itself a whole — an independent entity; and its relations to existence in general are misapprehended. Further, the size of the part as compared with the size of the whole must be misapprehended unless the whole is not only recognized as including it, but is figured in its total extent. And again, the position which the part occupies in relation to other parts cannot be rightly conceived unless there is some conception of the whole in its distribution as well as in its amount. Still more when part and whole, instead of being statically related only, are dynamically related, must there be a general understanding of the whole before the part can be understood. . . . Most of all, however, where the whole is organic does complete comprehension of a part imply extensive comprehension of the whole. Suppose a being ignorant of the human body to find a detached arm. If not misconceived by him as a supposed whole, instead of being conceived as a part, still its relation to other parts, and its structure, would be wholly inexplicable. . . . Conduct is a whole, and, in a sense, it is an organic whole — an aggregate of inter-dependent actions performed by an organism. That division or aspect of conduct with which ethics deals is a part of this organic whole — a part having its components inextricably bound up with the rest. . . . The whole of which ethics forms a part is the whole constituted by the theory of conduct in general;

and this whole must be understood before the part can be understood."

What is true of conduct is quite as true of art and literature. Just as without the conception of an ethical organism, we have no standard for the ethical evaluation of conduct, so without the conception of an æsthetic or a literary organism, we can have no standard for the evaluation of art or literature. The function of the parts, that is, of the various elements and devices of rhetoric such as figures, sentences, paragraphs, and composition generally, is inexplicable, or misapprehended, until they are given their proper place in the operation of the whole. Just what this whole, this organism in its detailed structure and function, is, cannot here be discussed at length. It is enough to say that as the content of ethics embraces all conduct in which there is adjustment of acts to ends, so the content of any adequate theory of style must embrace all manner of expression in which there is adjustment of utterance to comprehension. The literary organism, therefore, if we carry out the analogy, will be the whole complex of effective expression going on at any one time, the value of any part to be determined by the work which that part performs in the service of the whole.

If with this conception in mind we turn now to Spencer's theory of economy as outlined in his essay, we see at once the desirability of giving to his central principle an interpretation much wider than that which has been generally accepted. As commonly conceived from a reading of the essay, the principle of economy is in brief as follows:— Thought cannot be conveyed from one individual to another save through an apparatus of symbols, to apprehend which requires some mental effort. Whatever energy, therefore, can be saved in interpreting the symbols, goes to the apprehension of the thought. The effectiveness of language as a bearer of thought is thus measured by the ease with which

it gives up its contained idea.[1] In other words, the value
of style is determined by a kind of ledger account in which
so much mental energy is credited to idea, so much debited
to the bearer of the idea. All that is saved from the wages
of the bearer goes to swell the credit account. Or to put
the same thing in still another way, the cheaper the cost
of transmission, the larger the bulk of freight. The principle is an exceedingly simple one and readily applicable to
all forms of expression; but a little reflection will show
that, taken as it stands, without proper reference to social
conditions, it not only furnishes no sure standard of literary evaluation, but may even be at times positively
misleading. This will appear from the following consider-
ations. There are two kinds of economy: first, mere saving, the laying up of capital by isolated individuals without
purpose beyond bare accumulation; second, true economy,
which consists in wise expenditure and investment of all
that is accumulated. The first may be economy, it may be
miserliness, or it may be dead loss; no one can tell which.
So long as the individual is viewed as isolated, no standard
can be applied. Just so with Spencer's principle. Considering men as separate individuals whose relation one to
another is of an accidental character, one cannot say
whether the language they use is economical or otherwise.
What seems to be economy, may be a positive waste of
breath. To take an example. By a suitable choice of
words and a proper arrangement of sentences, a demagogue

---

[1] " The general theory set forth is, that effectiveness of style depends on
a choice of words and forms of sentence offering the least resistance to
thought in the mind of the reader or hearer — a foreshadowing of the general law of the ' line of least resistance ' as applied to the interpretation
of psychological phenomena, as well as phenomena in general."—' Spencer
and Evolution,' by E. L. Youmans, *Pop. Sci. Mo.*, Vol. 6, p. 28. But the
' line of least resistance,' unless it means the path of a part performing its
function in the service of the whole organism, has no normative significance.

may 'economize' the mental energies of his audience to
the last degree; and yet all the saving that he effects may,
in the truest sense, be considered so much dead loss.

If, however, we may conceive of an organism — an
organic whole—in which it is possible for each individual
to perform his proper function, the second and the true conception of economy becomes not only possible but necessary.
Each man then economizes to the utmost only when he sub-
serves the interest of the whole. True economy in this
case, as in the case of an industrial organization, means
perfect division of labor, intelligent co-operation and free
exchange of commodities. Whether any given expression
is an example of economy or of waste must be determined
by inquiring what service it performs in maintaining the
integrity of the organism, that is, in furthering the intellectual life of the whole community. This fundamental principle, once established, might be developed in its
details so as to show its operation in every possible mode
of literary expression. It could be applied as an instrument of criticism and interpretation to literature of any
time and any place. And it would seem to have this
advantage over any theory of style which has yet been
advanced: it would be based, as Mr. Spencer would desire,
upon the conception of an organic whole made up of
mutually dependent members, not upon a part misconceived as a whole, nor yet (as is the case with so many
critical doctrines) upon dead formulas and abstract generalizations, gathered indiscriminately from the wreckage of
out-worn theories.[1]

---

[1] See Bosanquet's remarks on the law of economy, 'History of Æsthetic,'
pp. 386-7.

THE PHILOSOPHY OF STYLE.

PART I.

CAUSES OF FORCE IN LANGUAGE WHICH DEPEND UPON ECONOMY OF THE MENTAL ENERGIES.

i. *The Principle of Economy.*

1. Commenting on the seeming incongruity between his father's argumentative powers and his ignorance of formal logic, Tristram Shandy says: — "It was a matter of just wonder with my worthy tutor, and two or three fellows of that learned society, that a man who knew not so much as the names of his tools, should be able to work after that fashion with them." Sterne's intended implication that a knowledge of the principles of reasoning neither makes, nor is essential to, a good reasoner, is doubtless true. Thus, too, is it with grammar. As Dr. Latham, condemning the usual school-drill in Lindley Murray, rightly remarks: — "Gross vulgarity is a fault to be prevented; but the proper prevention is to be got from habit — not rules." Similarly, there can be little question that good composition is far less dependent upon acquaintance with its laws, than upon practice and natural aptitude. A clear head, a quick imagination, and a sensitive ear, will go far towards making all rhetorical precepts needless. He who daily hears and reads well-framed sentences, will naturally more or less tend to use similar ones. And where there exists any mental

1

idiosyncrasy — where there is a deficient verbal memory, or an inadequate sense of logical dependence, or but little perception of order, or a lack of constructive ingenuity ; no amount of instruction will remedy the defect. Nevertheless, *some* practical result may be expected from a familiarity with the principles of style. The endeavour to conform to laws may tell, though slowly. And if in no other way, yet, as facilitating revision, a knowledge of the thing to be achieved — a clear idea of what constitutes a beauty, and what a blemish — cannot fail to be of service.

2. No general theory of expression seems yet to have been enunciated.[1] The maxims contained in works on composition and rhetoric, are presented in an unorganized form. Standing as isolated dogmas — as empirical generalizations, they are neither so clearly apprehended, nor so much respected, as they would be were they deduced from some simple first principle. We are told that "brevity is the soul of wit." We hear styles condemned as verbose or involved. Blair says that every needless part of a sentence "interrupts the description and clogs the image;" and again, that "long sentences fatigue the reader's attention."[2] It is remarked by Lord Kaimes, that "to give the utmost force to a period, it ought, if possible, to be closed with that word which makes the greatest figure."[3] That parentheses should be avoided and that Saxon words should be used in preference to those of Latin origin, are established precepts. But, however influential the truths thus dogmatically embodied, they would be much more influential if reduced to something like scientific ordination. In this, as in other cases, conviction will be greatly strengthened when we

---

[1] That is, in works purporting to be rhetorics. General theories of literary expression had been put forth by Goethe, Schiller, Schlegel, Schopenhauer, Hegel, Vischer, and many other writers on æsthetics.

[2] ' Lectures on Rhetoric and Belles Lettres,' Lect. xi.

[3] ' Elements of Criticism,' Chap. 18, § 2.

understand the *why.* And we may be sure that a comprehension of the general principle from which the rules of composition result, will not only bring them home to us with greater force, but will discover to us other rules of like origin.

3. On seeking for some clue to the law underlying these current maxims, we may see shadowed forth in many of them, the importance of economizing the reader's or hearer's attention. To so present ideas that they may be apprehended with the least possible mental effort, is the desideratum towards which most of the rules above quoted point. When we condemn writing that is wordy, or confused, or intricate — when we praise this style as easy, and blame that as fatiguing, we consciously or unconsciously assume this desideratum as our standard of judgment. Regarding language as an apparatus of symbols for the conveyance of thought,[1] we may say that, as in a mechanical apparatus, the more simple and the better arranged its parts, the greater will be the effect produced. In either case, whatever force is absorbed by the machine is deducted from the result. A reader or listener has at each moment but a limited amount of mental power available. To recognize and interpret the symbols presented to him, requires part of this power; to arrange and combine the images suggested requires a further part; and only that part which remains can be used for realizing the thought conveyed. Hence, the more time and attention it takes to receive and understand each sentence, the less time and attention can be given to the contained idea; and the less vividly will that idea be conceived.

4. How truly language must be regarded as a hindrance to thought, though the necessary instrument of it, we shall clearly perceive on remembering the comparative force with

---

[1] See the comment made by Mr. Wright, *infra,* § 13: "The definite product language is more or less isolated from the agency using it, and viewed more in relation to the reader's than the writer's mind." A brief criticism of the general principle will be found in A. S. Hill's 'Rhetoric,' pp. 163, 164.

which simple ideas are communicated by signs.[1] To say, "Leave the room," is less expressive than to point to the door. Placing a finger on the lips is more forcible than whispering, "Do not speak." A beck of the hand is better than, "Come here." No phrase can convey the idea of surprise so vividly as opening the eyes and raising the eyebrows. A shrug of the shoulders would lose much by translation into words. Again, it may be remarked that when oral language is employed, the strongest effects[2] are produced by interjections, which condense entire sentences into syllables. And in other cases, where custom allows us to express thoughts by single words, as in *Beware, Heigho, Fudge,* much force would be lost by expanding them into specific propositions. Hence, carrying out the metaphor that language is the vehicle of thought, there seems reason to think that in all cases the friction and inertia of the vehicle deduct from its efficiency; and that in composition, the chief, if not the sole thing to be done, is, to reduce this friction and inertia to the smallest possible amount. Let us then inquire whether economy of the recipient's attention is not the secret of effect, alike in the right choice and collocation of words, in the best arrangement of clauses in a sentence, in the proper order of its principal and subordinate propositions, in the judicious use of simile, metaphor, and other figures of speech, and even in the rhythmical sequence of syllables.

[1] This ingenious paradox rests upon an artificial distinction between language and other modes of expression. Language itself is but a system of verbal signs. What Spencer says is therefore virtually this: "Language is an inferior form of expression for ideas which are more easily expressed by other kinds of signs." Language in one sense is indeed a "hindrance to the expression of thought," and properly so; it forces vague and ill-defined thought back upon itself, compelling it to assume the organized form requisite to ordered verbal expression.

[2] "Strongest effects" is vague to the last degree. There may be hundreds of strong effects of all shades of complexity; very obviously not all of them can be produced by interjections.

ii. *Economy in the Use of Words.*

5. The greater forcibleness of Saxon English, or rather non-Latin English, first claims our attention. The several special reasons assignable for this may all be reduced to the general reason — economy. The most important of them is early association. A child's vocabulary is almost wholly Saxon. He says, *I have,* not *I possess — I wish,* not *I desire;* he does not *reflect,* he *thinks;* he does not beg for *amusement,* but for *play;* he calls things *nice* or *nasty,* not *pleasant* or *disagreeable.* The synonyms which he learns in after years, never become so closely, so organically connected with the ideas signified, as do these original words used in childhood; and hence the association remains less strong. But in what does a strong association between a word and an idea differ from a weak one? Simply in the greater ease and rapidity of the suggestive action. It can be in nothing else. Both of two words, if they be strictly synonymous, eventually call up the same image. The expression — It is *acid,* must in the end give rise to the same thought as — It is *sour;* but because the term *acid* was learnt later in life, and has not been so often followed by the thought symbolized, it does not so readily arouse that thought as the term *sour.* If we remember how slowly and with what labour the appropriate ideas follow unfamiliar words in another language, and how increasing familiarity with such words brings greater rapidity and ease of comprehension; and if we consider that the same process must have gone on with the words of our mother tongue from childhood upwards, we shall clearly see that the earliest learnt and oftenest used words, will, other things equal, call up images with less loss of time and energy than their later learnt synonyms.

6. The further superiority possessed by Saxon English in its comparative brevity, obviously comes under the same generalization. If it be an advantage to express an idea in

the smallest number of words, then will it be an advantage
to express it in the smallest number of syllables. If circui-
tous phrases and needless expletives distract the attention
and diminish the strength of the impression produced, then
do surplus articulations do so. A certain effort, though commonly an inappreciable one, must be required to recognize
every vowel and consonant. If, as all know, it is tiresome
to listen to an indistinct speaker, or read a badly-written
manuscript; and if, as we cannot doubt, the fatigue is a
cumulative result of the attention needed to catch successive syllables; it follows that attention is in such cases
absorbed by each syllable. And if this be true when the
syllables are difficult of recognition, it will also be true,
though in a less degree, when the recognition of them is
easy. Hence, the shortness of Saxon words becomes a reason for their greater force. One qualification, however,
must not be overlooked. A word which in itself embodies
the most important part of the idea to be conveyed, especially when that idea is an emotional one, may often with
advantage be a polysyllabic word. Thus it seems more
forcible to say, " It is *magnificent*," than " It is *grand*."
The word *vast* is not so powerful a one as *stupendous*. Calling a thing *nasty* is not so effective as calling it *disgusting*.

7. There seem to be several causes for this exceptional
superiority of certain long words. We may ascribe it
partly to the fact that a voluminous, mouth-filling epithet
is, by its very size, suggestive of largeness or strength;
witness the immense pomposity of sesquipedalian verbiage :
and when great power or intensity has to be suggested, this
association of ideas aids the effect. A further cause may be
that a word of several syllables admits of more emphatic
articulation; and as emphatic articulation is a sign of emotion, the unusual impressiveness of the thing named is implied by it. Yet another cause is that a long word (of
which the latter syllables are generally inferred as soon as

the first are spoken) allows the hearer's consciousness a
longer time to dwell upon the quality predicated; and
where, as in the above cases, it is to this predicated quality
that the entire attention is called, an advantage results
from keeping it before the mind for an appreciable time.
The reasons which we have given for preferring short words
evidently do not hold here. So that to make our generalization quite correct we must say, that while in certain
sentences expressing strong feeling, the word which more
especially implies that feeling may often with advantage
be a many-syllabled or Latin one; in the immense majority
of cases, each word serving but as a step to the idea embodied by the whole sentence, should, if possible, be a one-
syllabled or Saxon one.

8. Once more, that frequent cause of strength in Saxon
and other primitive words — their imitative character, may
be similarly resolved into the more general cause. Both
those directly imitative, as *splash, bang, whiz, roar,* &c., and
those analogically imitative, as *rough, smooth, keen, blunt,
thin, hard, crag,* &c., have a greater or less likeness to the
things symbolized; and by making on the senses impressions allied to the ideas to be called up, they save part of
the effort needed to call up such ideas, and leave more
attention for the ideas themselves.

9. The economy of the recipient's mental energy, into
which are thus resolvable the several causes of the strength
of Saxon English, may equally be traced in the superiority
of specific over generic words. That concrete terms produce more vivid impressions than abstract ones, and should,
when possible, be used instead, is a thorough maxim of
composition.[1] As Dr. Campbell says,[2] "The more general

---

[1] The purpose of the writer and the needs of the reader must, however,
always be taken into account. If the author's idea is such as to call for
abstract terms, concrete expressions are obviously out of place. Of the two
examples that follow in the text, it may be questioned whether to the legal
or scientific mind the first will not convey by far the greater satisfaction.

[2] ' Philosophy of Rhetoric,' Bk. III., Chap. 1, § 1.

the terms are, the picture is the fainter; the more special
they are, 'tis the brighter." We should avoid such a sentence as : — "In proportion as the manners, customs, and
amusements of a nation are cruel and barbarous, the regula-
tions of their penal code will be severe." And in place of
it we should write : — " In proportion as men delight in battles, bull-fights, and combats of gladiators, will they punish
by hanging, burning, and the rack." [1]

10. This superiority of specific expressions is clearly due
to a saving of the effort required to translate words into
thoughts. As we do not think in generals but in particulars — as, whenever any class of things is referred to, we
represent it to ourselves by calling to mind individual members of it; it follows that when an abstract word is used,
the hearer or reader has to choose from his stock of images,
one or more, by which he may figure to himself the genus
mentioned. In doing this, some delay must arise — some
force be expended; and if, by employing a specific term, an
appropriate image can be at once suggested, an economy is
achieved, and a more vivid impression produced. [2]

[1] Dr. Campbell's illustration is more to the point: "'Consider,' says
our Lord, 'the lilies how they grow: they toil not, they spin not; and yet
I say unto you, that Solomon in all his glory was not arrayed like one
of these. If, then, God so clothe the grass which to-day is in the field and
to-morrow is cast into the oven, how much more will he clothe you?' Let
us here adopt a little of the tasteless manner of modern paraphrasts, by
the substitution of more general terms, one of their many expedients of
infrigidating, and let us observe the effect produced by this change. 'Consider the flowers how they gradually increase in their size; they do no
manner of work, and yet I declare to you that no king whatever, in his
most splendid habit is dressed up like them. If, then, God in his provi-
dence doth so adorn the vegetable productions which continue but a little
time on the land, and are afterwards put into the fire, how much more will
he provide clothing for you?' How spiritless is the same sentiment ren-
dered by these small variations! The very particularizing of to-day and
to-morrow is infinitely more expressive of transitoriness than any description wherein the terms are general that can be substituted in its room."
— 'Philosophy of Rhetoric,' Bk. III., Chap. 1, § 1.

[2] The psychology of this passage is not above suspicion. The operation

iii. *The Principle of Economy applied to Sentences.*

11. Turning now from the choice of words to their sequence, we shall find the same general principle hold good.[1] We have *a priori* reasons for believing that in every sentence there is some one order of words more effective than any other; and that this order is the one which presents the elements of the proposition in the succession in which they may be most readily put together. As in a narrative, the events should be stated in such sequence that the mind may not have to go backwards and forwards in order to rightly connect them; as in a group of sentences, the arrangement should be such, that each of them may be understood as it comes, without waiting for subsequent ones; so in every sentence, the sequence of words should be that which suggests the constituents of the thought in the order most convenient for the building up that thought. Duly to enforce this truth, and to prepare the way for applications of it, we must briefly inquire into the mental act by which the meaning of a series of words is apprehended.[2]

of the mind in thinking a class is different from its operation in thinking a particular of that class. In the latter case the mental procedure consists in bringing up a particular image of the thing; in the former the mind grasps the function of the image, leaving the particular features wholly out of account. The trained thinker in thinking the class 'horse' does not "choose from his stock" of mental horses. He thinks the concept horse, and in so doing he may attain to a perfectly definite notion of the class without having in consciousness any particular horse whatsoever. The particular image is of course present, but such features as hight, color, etc., are simply disregarded. See, on this point, Dewey's 'Psychology,' pp. 204–213; James's 'Psychology,' I., Chap. 12; 'How do Concepts arise from Percepts?' by J. Dewey, in *Public School Journal* for November, 1891; James's address in Psychol. Rev.

[1] On the general question of the order of words in sentences, see the admirable little treatise by H. Weil, 'The Order of Words in the Ancient Languages compared with that of the Modern Languages' (Trans. by C. W. Super, Boston: 1887).

[2] "But there is another element we have to take into account, and that is the rhythmical effect of Style. Mr. Herbert Spencer in his essay very

12. We cannot more simply do this than by considering the proper collocation of the substantive and adjective. Is it better to place the adjective before the substantive, or the substantive before the adjective? Ought we to say with the French — *un cheval noir;* or to say as we do — a black horse? Probably, most persons of culture would decide that one order is as good as the other. Alive to the bias produced by habit, they would ascribe to that the preference they feel for our own form of expression. They would expect those educated in the use of the opposite form to have an equal preference for that. And thus they would conclude that neither of these instinctive judgments is of any worth. There is, however, a philosophical ground for deciding in favour of the English custom. If "a horse black" be the arrangement, immediately on the utterance of the word "horse," there arises, or tends to arise, in the mind, a picture answering to that word; and as there has been nothing to indicate what *kind* of horse, any image of a horse suggests itself. Very likely, however, the image will be that of a brown horse, brown horses being the most familiar. The result is that when the word "black" is added, a check is given to the process of thought. Either the picture of a brown horse already present to the imagination has to be suppressed, and the picture of a black one summoned in its place; or else, if the picture of a brown

clearly states the law of Sequence, but I infer that he would include it entirely under the law of Economy; at any rate he treats of it solely in reference to intelligibility, and not at all in its scarcely less important relation to harmony. . . . But Style appeals to the emotions as well as to the intellect, and the arrangement of words and sentences which will be the most economical may not be the most musical, and the most musical may not be the most pleasurably effective. For Climax and Variety it may be necessary to sacrifice something of rapid intelligibility: hence involutions, antitheses, and suspensions, which disturb the most orderly arrangement, may yet, in virtue of their own subtle influences, be counted as improvements on that arrangement." — Lewes's 'Principles of Success in Literature,' p. 143.

horse be yet unformed, the tendency to form it has to be stopped. Whichever is the case, a certain amount of hindrance results. But if, on the other hand, "a black horse" be the expression used, no such mistake can be made. The word "black," indicating an abstract quality, arouses no definite idea. It simply prepares the mind for conceiving some object of that colour; and the attention is kept suspended until that object is known. If, then, by the precedence of the adjective, the idea is conveyed without liability to error, whereas the precedence of the substantive is apt to produce a misconception, it follows that the one gives the mind less trouble than the other, and is therefore more forcible.[1]

13. Possibly it will be objected that the adjective and substantive come so close together, that practically they may be considered as uttered at the same moment; and that on hearing the phrase, "a horse black," there is not time to imagine a wrongly-coloured horse before the word "black" follows to prevent it. It must be owned that it is not easy to decide by introspection whether this is so or not.[2] But there are facts collaterally implying that it is not. Our

---

[1] Two fallacies lurk in this argument: (1) That the "bias produced by habit" is a factor that may be disregarded, for obviously if the substantive-adjective order were the one habitually employed and expected, economy would dictate that the opposite order be avoided; (2) that the particulars of a concrete visual image necessarily arise in the mind upon hearing the term 'horse.' The 'image' may be a sound or a moving line. "Take the following report from one of my students: 'I am unable to form in my mind's eye any visual likeness of the table whatever. After many trials I can only get a hazy surface, with nothing on or about it. I can see no variety in color, and no positive limitations in extent, while I cannot see what I see well enough to determine its position in respect to my eye, or to endow it with any quality of size. I am in the same position as to the word *dog*. I cannot see it in my mind's eye at all; and so cannot tell whether I should have to run my eye along it, if I did see it.'" —James's 'Psychology,' II., p. 57, note. The whole chapter should be read.

[2] See, for a discussion of this point, Victor Egger's 'La Parole intérieure,' Chaps. 6, 7; James's 'Psychology,' I., pp. 280, 281, note.

ability to anticipate the words yet unspoken is one of them. If the ideas of the hearer kept considerably behind the expressions of the speaker, as the objection assumes, he could hardly foresee the end of a sentence by the time it was half delivered: yet this constantly happens.[1] Were the supposition true, the mind, instead of anticipating, would be continually falling more and more in arrear. If the meanings of words are not realized as fast as the words are uttered, then the loss of time over each word must entail such an accumulation of delays as to leave a hearer entirely behind. But whether the force of these replies be or be not admitted, it will scarcely be denied that the right formation of a picture will be facilitated by presenting its elements in the order in which they are wanted;[2] even though the mind should do nothing until it has received them all.

14. What is here said respecting the succession of the adjective and substantive is obviously applicable, by change of terms, to the adverb and verb. And without further explanation, it will be manifest, that in the use of prepositions and other particles, most languages spontaneously conform with more or less completeness to this law.

---

[1] Spencer fails to see how this fact tells against his theory. (1) The Frenchman, accustomed to the substantive-adjective order, will anticipate the coming *noir*, or some other adjective, as soon as he hears the word *cheval*. Hence in his case the nascent image of a wrongly-colored horse will not tend to arise. The peculiar intonation of the substantive will probably give him a hint as to whether the adjective is or is not to follow. (2) In the case of the Englishman, the word ' black ' may lead the hearer to anticipate some other substantive than ' horse '; he may expect ' sheep,' or ' man,' or ' eye,' to follow, since all these things may possess the quality blackness.

[2] In the original article as it appeared in the *Westminster Review*, the following words are inserted at this point: " and that, as in forming the image answering to a red flower, the notion of redness is one of the components that must be used in the construction of the image, the mind, if put in possession of this notion before the specific image to be formed out of it is suggested, will more easily form it than if the order be reversed."

15. On applying a like analysis to the larger divisions of a sentence, we find not only that the same principle holds good, but that the advantage of respecting it becomes marked. In the arrangement of predicate and subject, for example, we are at once shown that as the predicate determines the aspect under which the subject is to be conceived, it should be placed first; and the striking effect produced by so placing it becomes comprehensible. Take the often-quoted contrast between " Great is Diana of the Ephesians," and " Diana of the Ephesians is great." When the first arrangement is used, the utterance of the word "great " arouses those vague associations of an impressive nature with which it has been habitually connected; the imagination is prepared to clothe with high attributes whatever follows; and when the words, "Diana of the Ephesians," are heard, all the appropriate imagery which can, on the instant, be summoned, is used in the formation of the picture: the mind being thus led directly, and without error, to the intended impression. When, on the contrary, the reverse order is followed, the idea, "Diana of the Ephesians," is conceived with no special reference to greatness; and when the words " is great " are added, the conception has to be remodelled : whence arises a loss of mental energy and a corresponding diminution of effect. The following verse from Coleridge's ' Ancient Mariner,' though somewhat irregular in structure, well illustrates the same truth :

> " *Alone, alone, all, all alone,*
> *Alone on a wide, wide sea !*
> And never a saint took pity on
> My soul in agony."

16. Of course the principle equally applies when the predicate is a verb or a participle. And as effect is gained by placing first all words indicating the quality, conduct or condition of the subject, it follows that the copula also should have precedence. It is true that the general habit

of our language resists this arrangement of predicate, copula and subject; but we may readily find instances of the additional force gained by conforming to it. Thus, in the line from 'Julius Cæsar' —

"'Then *burst* his mighty heart,"

priority is given to a word embodying both predicate and copula. In a passage contained in 'The Battle of Flodden Field,' the like order is systematically employed with great effect:

> "The Border slogan rent the sky !
> *A Home ! a Gordon ! was* the cry ;
> *Loud were* the clanging blows:
> *Advanced — forced back — now low, now high,*
> The pennon sunk and rose ;
> As *bends* the bark's mast in the gale
> When *rent are* rigging, shrouds and sail,
> It wavered 'mid the foes."

17. Pursuing the principle yet further, it is obvious that for producing the greatest effect, not only should the main divisions of a sentence observe this sequence, but the subdivisions of these should be similarly arranged. In nearly all cases, the predicate is accompanied by some limit or qualification, called its complement. Commonly, also, the circumstances of the subject, which form its complement, have to be specified. And as these qualifications and circumstances must determine the mode in which the acts and things they belong to are conceived, precedence should be given to them. Lord Kaimes[1] notices the fact that this order is preferable; though without giving the reason. He says : — " When a circumstance is placed at the beginning of the period, or near the beginning, the transition from it to the principal subject is agreeable : it is like ascending or going upward." A sentence arranged in illustration of this

---

1 'Elements of Criticism,' Chap. 18, § 2.

will be desirable. Here is one : — "Whatever it may be in theory, it is clear that in practice the French idea of liberty is — the right of every man to be master of the rest."

18. In this case, were the first two clauses, up to the word " practice " inclusive, which qualify the subject, to be placed at the end instead of the beginning, much of the force would be lost; as thus : — " The French idea of liberty is — the right of every man to be master of the rest; in practice at least, if not in theory."

19. Similarly with respect to the conditions under which any fact is predicated. Observe in the following example the effect of putting them last : — " How immense would be the stimulus to progress, were the honour now given to wealth and title given exclusively to high achievements and intrinsic worth ! "

20. And then observe the superior effect of putting them first : — " Were the honour now given to wealth and title given exclusively to high achievements and intrinsic worth, how immense would be the stimulus to progress ! "

21. The effect of giving priority to the complement of the predicate, as well as the predicate itself, is finely displayed in the opening of ' Hyperion ' :

> " *Deep in the shady sadness of a vale*
> *Far sunken from the healthy breath of morn,*
> *Far from the fiery noon and eve's one star*
> *Sat* gray-haired Saturn, quiet as a stone."

Here it will be observed, not only that the predicate " sat " precedes the subject "Saturn," and that the three lines in italics, constituting the complement of the predicate, come before it; but that in the structure of that complement also, the same order is followed: each line being so arranged that the qualifying words are placed before the words suggesting concrete images.

22. The right succession of the principal and subordinate propositions in a sentence manifestly depends on the same

law. Regard for economy of the recipient's attention,
which, as we find, determines the best order for the subject,
copula, predicate and their complements, dictates that the
subordinate proposition shall precede the principal one when
the sentence includes two. Containing, as the subordinate
proposition does, some qualifying or explanatory idea, its
priority prevents misconception of the principal one; and
therefore saves the mental effort needed to correct such
misconception. This will be seen in the annexed example:[1]
"The secrecy once maintained in respect to the parliamentary debates, is still thought needful in diplomacy; and in
virtue of this secret diplomacy, England may any day be
unawares betrayed by its ministers into a war costing a
hundred thousand lives, and hundreds of millions of treas-
ure: yet the English pique themselves on being a self-gov-
erned people." The two subordinate propositions, ending
with the semicolon and colon respectively, almost wholly
determine the meaning of the principal proposition with
which it concludes; and the effect would be lost were they
placed last instead of first.

23. The general principle of right arrangement in sentences, which we have traced in its application to the leading divisions of them, equally determines the proper order
of their minor divisions. In every sentence of any complexity the complement to the subject contains several
clauses, and that to the predicate several others; and these
may be arranged in greater or less conformity to the law of
easy apprehension. Of course with these, as with the
larger members, the succession should be from the less
specific to the more specific — from the abstract to the concrete.

---

[1] The following is the example given in the *Westminster Review:* "Those
who weekly go to church, and there have doled out to them a quantum of
belief which they have not energy to work out for themselves, are simply
spiritual paupers."

24. Now, however, we must notice a further condition to be fulfilled in the proper construction of a sentence; but still a condition dictated by the same general principle with the other: the condition, namely, that the words and expressions most nearly related in thought shall be brought the closest together. Evidently the single words, the minor clauses, and the leading divisions of every proposition, severally qualify each other. The longer the time that elapses between the mention of any qualifying member and the member qualified, the longer must the mind be exerted in carrying forward the qualifying member ready for use. And the more numerous the qualifications to be simultaneously remembered and rightly applied, the greater will be the mental power expended, and the smaller the effect produced. Hence, other things equal, force will be gained by so arranging the members of a sentence that these suspensions shall at any moment be the fewest in number; and shall also be of the shortest duration. The following is an instance of defective combination: — "A modern newspaper-statement, though probably true, would be laughed at if quoted in a book as testimony; but the letter of a court gossip is thought good historical evidence, if written some centuries ago." A rearrangement of this, in accordance with the principle indicated above, will be found to increase the effect. Thus: — "Though probably true, a modern newspaper-statement quoted in a book as testimony, would be laughed at; but the letter of a court gossip, if written some centuries ago, is thought good historical evidence."

25. By making this change, some of the suspensions are avoided and others shortened; while there is less liability to produce premature conceptions. The passage quoted below from 'Paradise Lost' affords a fine instance of a sentence well arranged; alike in the priority of the subordinate members, in the avoidance of long and numerous suspensions, and in the correspondence between the order

of the clauses and the sequence of the phenomena described, which, by the way, is a further prerequisite to easy comprehension, and therefore to effect.

> " As when a prowling wolf,
> Whom hunger drives to seek new haunt for prey,
> Watching where shepherds pen their flocks at eve,
> In hurdled cotes amid the field secure,
> Leaps o'er the fence with ease into the fold ;
> Or as a thief, bent to unhoard the cash
> Of some rich burgher, whose substantial doors,
> Cross-barr'd, and bolted fast, fear no assault,
> In at the window climbs, or o'er the tiles ;
> So clomb this first grand thief into God's fold ;
> So since into his church lewd hirelings climb." [1]

26. The habitual use of sentences in which all or most of the descriptive and limiting elements precede those described and limited, gives rise to what is called the inverted style: a title which is, however, by no means confined to this structure, but is often used where the order of the words is simply unusual. A more appropriate title would be the *direct style*, as contrasted with the other, or *indirect style:* the peculiarity of the one being, that it conveys each thought into the mind step by step with little liability to error; and of the other, that it gets the right thought conceived by a series of approximations.

27. The superiority of the direct over the indirect form of sentence, implied by the several conclusions that have been drawn, must not, however, be affirmed without reservation. Though, up to a certain point, it is well for the qualifying clauses of a period to precede those qualified; yet, as carrying forward each qualifying clause costs some mental effort, it follows that when the number of them and the time they are carried become great, we reach a limit beyond which more is lost than is gained. Other things equal, the

---

[1] Bk. IV., lines 183–193.

arrangement should be such that no concrete image shall be suggested until the materials out of which it is to be made have been presented. And yet, as lately pointed out, other things equal, the fewer the materials to be held at once, and the shorter the distance they have to be borne, the better. Hence in some cases it becomes a question whether most mental effort will be entailed by the many and long suspensions, or by the correction of successive misconceptions.

28. This question may sometimes be decided by considering the capacity of the persons addressed. A greater grasp of mind is required for the ready comprehension of thoughts expressed in the direct manner, where the sentences are anywise intricate. To recollect a number of preliminaries stated in elucidation of a coming- idea, and to apply them all to the formation of it when suggested, demands a good memory and considerable power of concentration. To one possessing these, the direct method will mostly seem the best; while to one deficient in them it will seem the worst. Just as it may cost a strong man less effort to carry a hundred-weight from place to place at once, than by a stone at a time; so, to an active mind it may be easier to bear along all the qualifications of an idea and at once rightly form it when named, than to first imperfectly conceive such idea and then carry back to it, one by one, the details and limitations afterwards mentioned. While conversely, as for a boy, the only possible mode of transferring a hundred-weight, is that of taking it in portions; so, for a weak mind, the only possible mode of forming a compound conception may be that of building it up by carrying separately its several parts.

29. That the indirect method — the method of conveying the meaning by a series of approximations — is best fitted for the uncultivated, may indeed be inferred from their habitual use of it. The form of expression adopted by the savage, as in — "Water, give me," is the simplest type of

the approximate arrangement. In pleonasms, which are comparatively prevalent among the uneducated, the same essential structure is seen; as, for instance, in — "The men, they were there." Again, the old possessive case — "The king, his crown," conforms to the like order of thought. Moreover, the fact that the indirect mode is called the natural one, implies that it is the one spontaneously employed by the common people: that is — the one easiest for undisciplined minds.

30. There are many cases, however, in which neither the direct nor the indirect structure is the best; but where an intermediate structure is preferable to both. When the number of circumstances and qualifications to be included in the sentence is great, the most judicious course is neither to enumerate them all before introducing the idea to which they belong, nor to put this idea first and let it be remodelled to agree with the particulars afterwards mentioned; but to do a little of each. Take a case. It is desirable to avoid so extremely indirect an arrangement as the following: — "We came to our journey's end, at last, with no small difficulty after much fatigue, through deep roads, and bad weather." Yet to transform this into an entirely direct sentence would not produce a satisfactory effect; as witness: — "At last, with no small difficulty, after much fatigue, through deep roads, and bad weather, we came to our journey's end."

31. Dr. Whately, from whom we quote the first of these two arrangements,[1] proposes this construction: — "At last, after much fatigue, through deep roads and bad weather, we came, with no small difficulty, to our journey's end." Here it will be observed that by introducing the words "we came" a little earlier in the sentence, the labour of carrying forward so many particulars is diminished, and the subsequent qualification "with no small difficulty" entails an

[1] 'Rhetoric,' Pt. III., Chap. 2, § 12.

addition to the thought that is very easily made. But a further improvement may be produced by introducing the words "we came" still earlier; especially if at the same time the qualifications be rearranged in conformity with the principle already explained, that the more abstract elements of the thought should come before the more concrete. Observe the better effect obtained by making these two changes : — " At last, with no small difficulty, and after much fatigue, we came, through deep roads and bad weather, to our journey's end." This reads with comparative smoothness ; that is, with less hindrance from suspensions and reconstructions of thought — with less mental effort.

32. Before dismissing this branch of our subject, it should be further remarked, that even when addressing the most vigorous intellects, the direct style is unfit for communicating ideas of a complex or abstract character. So long as the mind has not much to do, it may be well able to grasp all the preparatory clauses of a sentence, and to use them effectively ; but if some subtlety in the argument absorb the attention — if every faculty be strained in endeavouring to catch the speaker's or writer's drift, it may happen that the mind, unable to carry on both processes at once, will break down, and allow the elements of the thought to lapse into confusion.

iv. *The Principle of Economy applied to Figures.*

33. Turning now to consider figures of speech, we may equally discern the same general law of effect.[1] Underlying all the rules given for the choice and right use of them, we shall find the same fundamental requirement — economy of

---

[1] On the general subject of figures, see Max Müller's essay in *Fortnightly,* Vol. 46, p. 617, on 'Metaphor as a Mode of Abstraction'; Earle's 'English Prose,' pp. 234-253; Gummere's 'Poetics,' pp. 83-132; *Modern Language Notes,* Vol. 1, p. 140, 'The Classification of Rhetorical Figures,' by C. B. Bradley.

attention. It is indeed chiefly because they so well subserve this requirement, that figures of speech are employed.
To bring the mind more easily to the desired conception,
is in many cases solely, and in all cases mainly, their
object.

34. Let us begin with the figure called Synecdoche.
The advantage sometimes gained by putting a part for the
whole, is due to the more convenient, or more accurate,
presentation of the idea. If, instead of saying "a fleet of
ten ships," we say "a fleet of ten *sail*," the picture of a
group of vessels at sea is more readily suggested; and is so
because the sails constitute the most conspicuous parts of
vessels so circumstanced: whereas the word *ships* would
very likely remind us of vessels in dock. Again, to say,
" All *hands* to the pumps," is better than to say, " All *men*
to the pumps," as it suggests the men in the special attitude
intended, and so saves effort. Bringing "*gray hairs* with
sorrow to the grave," is another expression, the effect of
which has the same cause.

35. The occasional increase of force produced by Meton-
ymy may be similarly accounted for. "The low morality
of *the bar*," is a phrase both more brief and significant than
the literal one it stands for. A belief in the ultimate su-
premacy of intelligence over brute force, is conveyed in a
more concrete, and therefore more realizable form, if we
substitute *the pen* and *the sword* for the two abstract terms.
To say, " Beware of drinking! " is less effective than to say,
" Beware of *the bottle!* " and is so, clearly because it calls
up a less specific image.

36. The Simile is in many cases used chiefly with a view
to ornament, but whenever it increases the *force* of a passage, it does so by being an economy. Here in an instance :
" The illusion that great men and great events came oftener
in early times than now, is partly due to historical perspec-
tive. As in a range of equidistant columns, the furthest

off look the closest; so, the conspicuous objects of the past seem more thickly clustered the more remote they are."

37. To construct by a process of literal explanation, the thought thus conveyed would take many sentences, and the first elements of the picture would become faint while the imagination was busy in adding the others. _But by the help_ of a comparison all effort is saved; the picture is instantly realized, and its full effect produced.

38. Of the position of the Simile,[1] it needs only to remark, that what has been said respecting the order of the adjective and substantive, predicate and subject, principal and subordinate propositions, &c., is applicable here. _As whatever qualifies should precede whatever is qualified, force will generally be gained by placing the simile before_ the object to which it is applied. That this arrangement is the best, may be seen in the following passage from the 'Lady of the Lake':

> "As wreath of snow, on mountain breast,
> Slides from the rock that gave it rest,
> Poor Ellen glided from her stay,
> And at the monarch's feet she lay."[2]

Inverting these couplets will be found to diminish the effect considerably. There are cases, however, even where the simile is a simple one, in which it may with advantage be

---

[1] Properly the term "simile" is applicable only to the entire figure, inclusive of the two things compared and the comparison drawn between them. But as there exists no name for the illustrative member of the figure, there seems no alternative but to employ "simile" to express this also. This context will in each case show in which sense the word is used. — H. S.

[2] But compare the arrangement in the following from 'Othello':

> "Of one whose subdued eyes,
> Albeit unused to the melting mood
> Drop tears as fast as the Arabian trees
> Their medicinal gum."

placed last, as in these lines from Alexander Smith's 'Life Drama':

> " I see the future stretch
> All dark and barren as a rainy sea."

The reason for this seems to be, that so abstract an idea as that attaching to the word "future," does not present itself to the mind in any definite form, and hence the subsequent arrival at the simile entails no reconstruction of the thought.

39. Such, however, are not the only cases in which this order is the most forcible. As the advantage of putting the simile before the object depends on its being carried forward in the mind to assist in forming an image of the object, it must happen that if, from length or complexity, it cannot be so carried forward, the advantage is not gained. The annexed sonnet, by Coleridge, is defective from this cause:

> " As when a child, on some long winter's night,
> Affrighted, clinging to its grandam's knees,
> With eager wond'ring and perturb'd delight
> Listens strange tales of fearful dark decrees,
> Mutter'd to wretch by necromantic spell;
> Or of those hags who at the witching time
> Of murky midnight, ride the air sublime,
> And mingle foul embrace with fiends of hell;
> Cold horror drinks its blood! Anon the tear
> More gentle starts, to hear the beldame tell
> Of pretty babes, that lov'd each other dear,
> Murder'd by cruel uncle's mandate fell:
> Ev'n such the shiv'ring joys thy tones impart,
> Ev'n so, thou, Siddons, meltest my sad heart."

40. Here, from the lapse of time and accumulation of circumstances, the first part of the comparison is forgotten before its application is reached, and requires re-reading. Had the main idea been first mentioned, less effort would have been required to retain it, and to modify the conception of it into harmony with the comparison, than to remember the comparison, and refer back to its successive features for help in forming the final image.

41. The superiority of the Metaphor to the Simile is ascribed by Dr. Whately[1] to the fact that "all men are more gratified at catching the resemblance for themselves, than in having it pointed out to them." But after what has been said, the great economy it achieves will seem the more probable cause. Lear's exclamation —

> "Ingratitude ! thou marble-hearted fiend,"

would lose part of its effect were it changed into —

> "Ingratitude ! thou fiend with heart like marble ; "

and the loss would result partly from the position of the simile and partly from the extra number of words required. When the comparison is an involved one, the greater force ↖ of the metaphor, consequent on its greater brevity, becomes much more conspicuous. If, drawing an analogy between mental and physical phenomena, we say, "As, in passing through the crystal, beams of white light are decomposed into the colours of the rainbow ; so, in traversing the soul of the poet, the colourless rays of truth are transformed into brightly tinted poetry"; it is clear that in receiving the double set of words expressing the two halves of the comparison, and in carrying the one half to the other, considerable attention is absorbed. Most of this is saved, however, by putting the comparison in a metaphorical form, thus : "The white light of truth, in traversing the many sided transparent soul of the poet, is refracted into iris-hued poetry."

42. How much is conveyed in a few words by the help of the Metaphor, and how vivid the effect consequently produced, may be abundantly exemplified. From 'A Life Drama' may be quoted the phrase, -

> "I spear'd him with a jest,"

as a fine instance among the many which that poem con-

[1] 'Rhetoric,' Pt. III., Chap. 2, § 3.

tains. A passage in the 'Prometheus Unbound,' of Shelley, displays the power of the metaphor to great advantage:

> " Methought among the lawns together
> We wandered, underneath the young gray dawn,
> And multitudes of dense white fleecy clouds
> Were wandering, in thick flocks along the mountains
> *Shepherded* by the slow unwilling wind."

This last expression is remarkable for the distinctness with which it realizes the features of the scene: bringing the mind, as it were, by a bound to the desired conception.

43. But a limit is put to the advantageous use of the Metaphor, by the condition that it must be sufficiently simple to be understood from a hint. Evidently, if there be any obscurity in the meaning or application of it, no economy of attention will be gained; but rather the reverse. Hence, when the comparison is complex, it is usual to have recourse to the Simile. There is, however, a species of figure, sometimes classed under Allegory, but which might, perhaps, be better called Compound Metaphor, that enables us to retain the brevity of the metaphorical form even where the analogy is intricate. This is done by indicating the application of the figure at the outset, and then leaving the mind to continue the parallel.[1] Emerson has employed it with great effect in the first of his ' Lectures on the Times ': — "The main interest which any aspects of the Times can have for us, is the great spirit which gazes through them, the light which they can shed on the wonderful questions, What are we, and Whither we tend? We do not wish to be deceived. Here we drift, like white sail across the wild ocean, now bright on the wave, now darkling in the trough of the sea; but from what port did we sail? Who

[1] Not uncommon in Shakespeare, as, for example, the following from 'Hamlet,' IV., 2: — " But such officers do the king best service in the end: he keeps them, as an ape doth nuts, in the corner of his jaw; first mouth'd to be last swallowed."

knows? Or to what port are we bound? Who knows? There is no one to tell us but such poor weather-tossed mariners as ourselves, whom we speak as we pass, or who have hoisted some signal, or floated to us some letter in a bottle from far. But what know they more than we? They also found themselves on this wondrous sea. No; from the older sailors nothing. Over all their speaking trumpets the gray sea and the loud winds answer, Not in us; not in Time."

44. The division of the Simile from the Metaphor is by no means a definite one. Between the one extreme in which the two elements of the comparison are detailed at full length and the analogy pointed out, and the other extreme in which the comparison is implied instead of stated, come intermediate forms, in which the comparison is partly stated and partly implied. For instance : — "Astonished at the performances of the English plow, the Hindoos paint it, set it up, and worship it; thus turning a tool into an idol: linguists do the same with language." There is an evident advantage in leaving the reader or hearer to complete the figure. And generally these intermediate forms are good in proportion as they do this; provided the mode of completing it be obvious.

45. Passing over much that may be said of like purport upon Hyperbole, Personification, Apostrophe, &c., let us close our remarks upon construction by a typical example. The general principle which has been enunciated is, that other things equal, the force of all verbal forms and arrangements is great, in proportion as the time and mental effort they demand from the recipient is small. The corollaries from this general principle have been severally illustrated; and it has been shown that the relative goodness of any two modes of expressing an idea, may be determined by observing which requires the shortest process of thought for its comprehension. But though conformity in particu-

lar points has been exemplified, no cases of complete conformity have yet been quoted. It is indeed difficult to find
them; for the English idiom does not commonly permit
the order which theory dictates. A few, however, occur in
Ossian. Here is one: — "As autumn's dark storms pour
from two echoing hills, so towards each other approached
the heroes. As two dark streams from high rocks meet and
mix, and roar on the plain: loud, rough, and dark in battle
meet Lochlin and Inisfail. . . . As the troubled noise of
the ocean when roll the waves on high; as the last peal of
the thunder of heaven; such is noise of the battle."

46. Except in the position of the verb in the first two
similes, the theoretically best arrangement is fully carried
out in each of these sentences. The simile comes before
the qualified image, the adjectives before the substantives,
the predicate and copula before the subject, and their
respective complements before them. That the passage
is open to the charge of being bombastic proves nothing; or
rather, proves our case. For what is bombast but a force
of expression too great for the magnitude of the ideas
embodied? All that may rightly be inferred is, that only
in very rare cases, and then only to produce a climax, should
all the conditions of effective expression be fulfilled.

v. *Suggestion as a Means of Economy.*

47. Passing on to a more complex application of the
doctrine with which we set out, it must now be remarked,
that not only in the structure of sentences, and the use of
figures of speech, may economy of the recipient's mental
energy be assigned as the cause of force; but that in the
choice and arrangement of the minor images, out of which
some large thought is to be built up, we may trace the same
condition to effect. To select from the sentiment, scene, or
event, described those typical elements which carry many
others along with them; and so, by saying a few things

but suggesting many, to abridge the description; is the secret of producing a vivid impression.[1] An extract from Tennyson's 'Mariana' will well illustrate this:

> "All day within the dreamy house,
>   The door upon the hinges creaked,
>   The blue fly sung i' the pane ; the mouse
>   Behind the mouldering wainscot shrieked,
>   Or from the crevice peered about."

48. The several circumstances here specified bring with them many appropriate associations. Our attention is rarely drawn by the buzzing of a fly in the window, save when everything is still. While the inmates are moving about the house, mice usually keep silence; and it is only when extreme quietness reigns that they peep from their retreats. Hence each of the facts mentioned, presupposing numerous others, calls up these with more or less distinctness; and revives the feeling of dull solitude with which they are connected in our experience. Were all these facts detailed instead of suggested, the attention would be so frittered away that little impression of dreariness would be produced. Similarly in other cases. Whatever the nature of the thought to be conveyed, this skilful selection of a few particulars which imply the rest, is the key to success. In the choice of component ideas, as in the choice of expressions, the aim must be to convey the greatest quantity of thoughts with the smallest quantity of words.

49. The same principle may in some cases be advantageously carried yet further, by indirectly suggesting some entirely distinct thought in addition to the one expressed. Thus, if we say, "The head of a good classic is as full of ancient myths, as that of a servant-girl of ghost stories";

---

[1] The following sentence occurs at this point in the *Westminster Review* text:— "Thus if we say, Real nobility is 'not transferable'; besides the one idea expressed several are implied, and as these can be thought much sooner than they can be put in words, there is gain in omitting them."

it is manifest that besides the fact asserted, there is an implied opinion respecting the small value of classical knowledge: and as this implied opinion is recognized much sooner than it can be put into words, there is gain in omitting it. In other cases, again, great effect is produced by an overt omission; provided the nature of the idea left out is obvious. A good instance of this occurs in 'Heroes and Hero-worship.' After describing the way in which Burns was sacrificed to the idle curiosity of Lion-hunters — people who came not out of sympathy, but merely to *see* him — people who sought a little amusement, and who got their amusement while "the Hero's life went for it!" Carlyle suggests a parallel thus: "Richter says, in the Island of Sumatra there is a kind of 'Light-chafers,' large Fire-flies, which people stick upon spits, and illuminate the ways with at night. Persons of condition can thus travel with a pleasant radiance, which they much admire. Great honour to the Fire-flies! But —! —"

vi. *The Effect of Poetry explained.*

50. Before inquiring whether the law of effect, thus far traced, explains the superiority of poetry to prose, it will be needful to notice some supplementary causes of force in expression, that have not yet been mentioned. These are not, properly speaking, additional causes; but rather secondary ones, originating from those already specified — reflex results of them. In the first place, then, we may remark that mental excitement spontaneously prompts the use of those forms of speech which have been pointed out as the most effective. "Out with him!"[1] "Away with him!" are the natural utterances of angry citizens at a disturbed meeting. A voyager, describing a terrible storm he had witnessed, would rise to some such climax as — "Crack

---

[1] "Put him out!" is the form most commonly heard in this country.

went the ropes and down came the mast." Astonishment may be heard expressed in the phrase — "Never was there such a sight!" All of which sentences are, it will be observed, constructed after the direct type. Again, every one knows that excited persons are given to figures of speech. The vituperation of the vulgar abounds with them : often, indeed, consists of little else. "Beast," "brute," "gallows rogue," "cut-throat villain," these, and other like metaphors and metaphorical epithets, at once call to mind a street quarrel. Further, it may be noticed that extreme brevity is another characteristic of passionate language. The sentences are generally incomplete; the particles are omitted; and frequently important words are left to be gathered from the context. Great admiration does not vent itself in a precise proposition, as — "It is beautiful"; but in the simple exclamation, — "Beautiful!" He who, when reading a lawyer's letter, should say, "Vile rascal!" would be thought angry; while, "He is a vile rascal!" would imply comparative coolness. Thus we see that alike in the order of the words, in the frequent use of figures, and in extreme conciseness, the natural utterances of excitement conform to the theoretical conditions of forcible expression.

51. Hence, then, the higher forms of speech acquire a secondary strength from association. Having, in actual life, habitually heard them in connection with vivid mental impressions, and having been accustomed to meet with them in the most powerful writing, they come to have in themselves a species of force. The emotions that have from time to time been produced by the strong thoughts wrapped up in these forms, are partially aroused by the forms themselves. They create a certain degree of animation; they induce a preparatory sympathy, and when the striking ideas looked for are reached, they are the more vividly realized.

52. The continuous use of these modes of expressic that are alike forcible in themselves and forcible from their associations, produces the peculiarly impressive species of composition which we call poetry. Poetry, we shall find, habitually adopts those symbols of thought, and those methods of using them, which instinct and analysis agree in choosing as most effective, and becomes poetry by virtue of doing this. On turning back to the various specimens that have been quoted, it will be seen that the direct or inverted form of sentence predominates in them; and that to a degree quite inadmissible in prose. And not only in the frequency, but in what is termed the violence of the inversions, will this distinction be remarked. In the abundant use of figures, again, we may recognize the same truth. Metaphors, similes, hyperboles, and personifications, are the poet's colours, which he has liberty to employ almost without limit. We characterize as "poetical" the prose which uses these appliances of language with any frequency, and condemn it as "over florid" or "affected" long before they occur with the profusion allowed in verse. Further, let it be remarked that in brevity — the other requisite of forcible expression which theory points out, and emotion spontaneously fulfils — poetical phraseology similarly differs from ordinary phraseology. Imperfect periods are frequent; elisions are perpetual; and many of the minor words, which would be deemed essential in prose, are dispensed with.

53. Thus poetry, regarded as a vehicle of thought, is especially impressive partly because it obeys all the laws of effective speech, and partly because in so doing it imitates the natural utterances of excitement. While the matter embodied is idealized emotion, the vehicle is the idealized language of emotion. As the musical composer catches the cadences in which our feelings of joy and sympathy, grief and despair, vent themselves, and out of these germs evolves

melodies suggesting higher phases of these feelings;[1] so, the poet develops from the typical expressions in which men utter passion and sentiment, those choice forms of verbal combination in which concentrated passion and sentiment may be fitly presented.

54. There is one peculiarity of poetry conducing much to its effect — the peculiarity which is indeed usually thought its characteristic one — still remaining to be considered: we mean its rhythmical structure. This, improbable though it seems, will be found to come under the same generalization with the others. Like each of them, it is an idealization of the natural language of strong emotion, which is known to be more or less metrical if the emotion be not too violent; and like each of them it is an economy of the reader's or hearer's attention. In the peculiar tone and manner we adopt in uttering versified language, may be discerned its relationship to the feelings; and the pleasure which its measured movement gives us, is ascribable to the comparative ease with which words metrically arranged can be recognized.

55. This last position will scarcely be at once admitted; but a little explanation will show its reasonableness. For if, as we have seen, there is an expenditure of mental energy in the mere act of listening to verbal articulations, or in that silent repetition of them which goes on in reading[2] — if the perceptive faculties must be in active exercise to identify every syllable — then, any mode of so combining words as to present a regular recurrence of certain traits

[1] For Spencer's views on the relation of music to speech-tunes, see his essay on the 'Origin and Function of Music' in 'Essays, Scientific, Political, and Speculative'; his recent paper on the 'Origin of Music' in *Mind* for October, 1890; the discussion by R. Wallaschek and J. McK. Cattell in *Mind* for July, 1891; and Chap. 21 of Gurney's 'Power of Sound.'

[2] There has been much discussion over this point. See Bain, 'Senses and Intellect,' pp.345,353; Stricker, 'Studien über die Sprachvorstellungen'; *Revue Philosophique*, Vol. 16, p. 405; Vol. 18, p. 685; and Vol. 19, p. 118.

which the mind can anticipate, will diminish that strain
upon the attention required by the total irregularity of
prose.[1] Just as the body, in receiving a series of varying
concussions, must keep the muscles ready to meet the most
violent of them, as not knowing when such may come; so,
the mind in receiving unarranged articulations, must keep
its perceptives active enough to recognize the least easily
caught sounds. And as, if the concussions recur in a definite order, the body may husband its forces by adjusting the
resistance needful for each concussion; so, if the syllables
be rhythmically arranged, the mind may economize its
energies by anticipating the attention required for each
syllable.[2]

56. Far-fetched though this idea will perhaps be thought,
a little introspection will countenance it. That we *do* take
advantage of metrical language to adjust our perceptive
faculties to the force of the expected articulations, is clear
from the fact that we are balked by halting versification.
Much as at the bottom of a flight of stairs, a step more or
less than we counted upon gives us a shock; so, too, does a
misplaced accent or a supernumerary syllable. In the one
case, we *know* that there is an erroneous preadjustment;
and we can scarcely doubt that there is one in the other.
But if we habitually preadjust our perceptions to the measured movement of verse, the physical analogy above given
renders it probable that by so doing we economize atten-

[1] Good prose is far from being totally irregular. It has a large rhythm
peculiar to itself which is difficult to define, but even with an untrained
ear, easy to perceive. The day-laborer making his way through a news-
paper article will often complain that "the writing doesn't run smooth."
He means that the prose-rhythm is defective. Consult on this point,
Saintsbury's 'Specimens of English Prose Style,' Introduction; Steven-
son's essay on ' Style in Literature,' *Contemporary Review*, Vol. 47, p. 548;
Ellis's ' On the Physical Constituents of Accent and Emphasis ' in Transac-
tions of the English Philological Society for 1873–4, pp. 113–164.

[2] See Appendix A.

tion; and hence that metrical language is more effective than prose, because it enables us to do this.[1]

57. Were there space, it might be worth while to inquire whether the pleasure we take in rhyme, and also that which we take in euphony, are not partly ascribable to the same general cause.

[1] " What the rhythm of the dance is to our muscular energies, the rhythm of poetry and music is to the ear. Its main constituent as a pleasure is the regularity of its occurrence and the consequent possibility of relaxing our attention to the accentuation or the arrangement of chords. While syllables irregularly thrown together require a certain amount of jumping from point to point in the auditory perception, syllables placed in a regular order of short and long allow us to withdraw the attention from their accent and to expect a continuance of the same harmonious and easily followed succession. Many familiar facts concur to justify this explanation. In attempting for the first time to read a perfectly new metre, it is sometimes a few minutes before *we fall into the swing of it*, as we phrase it; that is, before our auditory apparatus accommodates itself to the new mode of recurrence." — Grant Allen, ' Physiological Æsthetics,' p. 115.

"The members or clauses and the periods themselves should be neither truncated nor too long. If they are too short, they often make a hearer stumble; for if, while he is hurrying on to the completion of the measure or rhythm, of which he has a definite notion in his mind, he is suddenly pulled up by a pause on the part of the speaker, there will necessarily follow a sort of stumble in consequence of the sudden check." — Aristotle, ' Rhetoric,' III. 9, Welldon's Trans.

PART II.

CAUSES OF FORCE IN LANGUAGE WHICH DEPEND UPON ECONOMY OF THE MENTAL SENSIBILITIES.

i. *The Law of Mental Exhaustion and Repair.*

58. A few paragraphs only, can be devoted to a second division of our subject that here presents itself. To pursue in detail the laws of effect, as applying to the larger features of composition, would carry us beyond our limits. But we may briefly indicate a further aspect of the general principle hitherto traced out, and hint a few of its wider applications.

59. Thus far, then, we have considered only those causes of force in language which depend upon economy of the mental *energies:* we have now to glance at those which depend upon economy of the mental *sensibilities.* Questionable though this division may be as a psychological one, it will yet serve roughly to indicate the remaining field of investigation. It will suggest that besides considering the extent to which any faculty or group of faculties is tasked in receiving a form of words and realizing its contained idea, we have to consider the state in which this faculty or group of faculties is left; and how the reception of subsequent sentences and images will be influenced by that state. Without going at length into so wide a topic as the exercise of faculties and its reactive effects, it will be sufficient here to call to mind that every faculty (when in a state of normal activity) is most capable at the outset; and that the change in its condition, which ends in what we term

exhaustion, begins simultaneously with its exercise. This generalization, with which we are all familiar in our bodily experiences, and which our daily language recognizes as true of the mind as a whole, is equally true of each mental power, from the simplest of the senses to the most complex of the sentiments. If we hold a flower to the nose for long, we become insensible to its scent. We say of a very brilliant flash of lightning that it blinds us; which means that our eyes have for a time lost their ability to appreciate light. After eating a quantity of honey, we are apt to think our tea is without sugar. The phrase "a deafening roar," implies that men find a very loud sound temporarily incapacitates them for hearing faint ones. To a hand which has for some time carried a heavy body, small bodies afterwards lifted seem to have lost their weight. Now, the truth at once recognized in these, its extreme manifestations, may be traced throughout. It may be shown that alike in the reflective faculties, in the imagination, in the perceptions of the beautiful, the ludicrous, the sublime, in the sentiments, the instincts, in all the mental powers, however we may classify them — action exhausts; and that in proportion as the action is violent, the subsequent prostration is great.

60. Equally, throughout the whole nature, may be traced the law that exercised faculties are ever tending to resume their original state. Not only after continued rest, do they regain their full power — not only do brief cessations partially reinvigorate them; but even while they are in action, the resulting exhaustion is ever being neutralized. The two processes of waste and repair go on together. Hence with faculties habitually exercised — as the senses of all persons, or the muscles of any one who is strong — it happens that, during moderate activity, the repair is so nearly equal to the waste, that the diminution of power is scarcely appreciable; and it is only when the activity has been long

continued, or has been very violent, that the repair becomes so far in arrear of the waste as to produce a perceptible prostration. In all cases, however, when, by the action of a faculty, waste has been incurred, *some* lapse of time must take place before full efficiency can be reacquired; and this time must be long in proportion as the waste has been great.[1]

ii. *Explanation of Climax, Antithesis, and Anticlimax.*

61. Keeping in mind these general truths, we shall be in a condition to understand certain causes of effect in composition now to be considered. Every perception received, and every conception realized, entailing some amount of waste — or, as Liebig would say, some change of matter in the brain; and the efficiency of the faculties subject to this waste-being thereby temporarily, though often but momentarily, diminished; the resulting partial inability must affect the acts of perception and conception that immediately succeed. And hence we may expect that the vividness with which images are realized will, in many cases, depend on the order of their presentation: even when one order is as convenient to the understanding as the other.

62. There are sundry facts which alike illustrate this, and are explained by it. Climax is one of them. The marked effect obtained by placing last the most striking of any series of images, and the weakness — often the ludicrous weakness — produced by reversing this arrangement, depends on the general law indicated. As immediately after looking at the sun we cannot perceive the light of a fire, while by looking at the fire first and the sun afterwards we can perceive both; so, after receiving a brilliant, or weighty, or terrible thought, we cannot appreciate a less brilliant,

[1] For an expansion of these ideas, with many examples, see **Grant Allen's** 'Physiological Æsthetics,' Chaps. 1, 2.

less weighty, or less terrible one, while, by reversing the order, we can appreciate each. In Antithesis, again, we may recognize the same general truth. The opposition of two thoughts that are the reverse of each other in some promi-⤶ nent trait, insures an impressive effect; and does this by giving a momentary relaxation to the faculties addressed. If, after a series of images of an ordinary character, appealing in a moderate degree to the sentiment of reverence, or approbation, or beauty, the mind has presented to it a very insignificant, a very unworthy, or a very ugly image; the faculty of reverence, or approbation, or beauty, as the case may be, having for the time nothing to do, tends to resume its full power; and will immediately afterwards appreciate a vast, admirable, or beautiful image better than it would otherwise do. Conversely, where the idea of absurdity due to extreme insignificance is to be produced, it may be greatly intensified by placing it after something highly impressive: especially if the form of phrase implies that something still more impressive is coming. A good illustration of the effect gained by thus presenting a petty idea to a consciousness that has not yet recovered from the shock of an exciting one, occurs in a sketch by Balzac. His hero writes to a mistress who has cooled towards him the following letter:

"MADAME, — Votre conduite m'étonne autant qu'elle m'afflige. Non contente de me déchirer le cœur par vos dédains, vous avez l'indélicatesse de me retenir une brosse à dents, que mes moyens ne me permettent pas de remplacer, mes propriétés étant grevées d'hypothèques.

"Adieu, trop belle et trop ingrate amie! Puissions-nous nous revoir dans un monde meilleur!

"CHARLES-EDOUARD."

63. Thus we see that the phenomena of Climax, Antithesis, and Anticlimax, alike result from this general principle.

Improbable as these momentary variations in susceptibility
may seem, we cannot doubt their occurrence when we con-
template the analogous variations in the susceptibility of the
senses. Referring once more to phenomena of vision, every
one knows that a patch of black on a white ground looks
blacker, and a patch of white on a black ground looks whiter,
than elsewhere. As the blackness and the whiteness must
really be the same, the only assignable cause for this is a
difference in their actions upon us, dependent upon the
different states of our faculties. It is simply a visual antithesis.[1]

iii. *Need of Variety.*

64. But this extension of the general principle of economy
— this further condition to effective composition, that the
sensitiveness of the faculties must be continuously hus-
banded — includes much more than has been yet hinted.
It implies not only that certain arrangements and certain
juxtapositions of connected ideas are best; but that some
modes of dividing and presenting a subject will be more
striking than others; and that, too, irrespective of its logical
cohesion. It shows why we must progress from the less
interesting to the more interesting; and why not only the
composition as a whole, but each of its successive portions,
should tend towards a climax. At the same time, it forbids
long continuity of the same kind of thought, or repeated
production of like effects. It warns us against the error
committed both by Pope in his poems and by Bacon in his
essays — the error, namely, of constantly employing forcible
forms of expression: and it points out that as the easiest
posture by and by becomes fatiguing, and is with pleasure
exchanged for one less easy, so, the most perfectly-con-

[1] On this point see Mr. E. B. Delabarre's paper on 'The Law of Contrast,' printed in James's ' Psychology,' II., pp. 13-27.

structed sentences will soon weary, and relief will be given by using those of an inferior kind.[1]

65. Further, we may infer from it not only that we should avoid generally combining our words in one manner, however good, or working out our figures and illustrations in one way, however telling; but that we should avoid anything like uniform adherence, even to the wider conditions of effect. We should not make every section of our subject progress in interest; we should not always rise to a climax. As we saw that, in single sentences, it is but rarely allowable to fulfil all the conditions to strength; so, in the larger sections of a composition we must not often conform entirely to the law indicated. We must subordinate the component effect to the total effect.

66. In deciding how practically to carry out the principles of artistic composition, we may derive help by bearing in mind a fact already pointed out — the fitness of certain verbal arrangements for certain kinds of thought. That constant variety in the mode of presenting ideas which the theory demands, will in a great degree result from a skilful adaptation of the form to the matter. We saw how the direct or inverted sentence is spontaneously used by excited people; and how their language is also characterized by figures of speech and by extreme brevity. Hence these may with advantage predominate in emotional passages; and may increase as the emotion rises. On the other hand, for complex ideas, the indirect sentence seems the best vehicle. In conversation, the excitement produced by the near approach to a desired conclusion, will often show itself in a series of short, sharp sentences; while, in impressing a view already enunciated, we generally make our periods voluminous by

---

[1] But why, if they accomplish their purpose, should they be looked upon as 'inferior'? Surely, the 'perfectly constructed' sentence is the one which fulfils its purpose on a particular occasion and in a particular connection.

piling thought upon thought. These natural modes of procedure may serve as guides in writing. Keen observation and skilful analysis would, in like manner, detect further peculiarities of expression produced by other attitudes of mind; and by paying due attention to all such traits, a writer possessed of sufficient versatility might make some approach to a completely-organized work.

iv. *The Ideal Writer.*

67. This species of composition which the law of effect points out as the perfect one, is the one which high genius tends naturally to produce. As we found that the kinds of sentences which are theoretically best, are those generally employed by superior minds, and by inferior minds when excitement has raised them; so, we shall find that the ideal form for a poem, essay, or fiction, is that which the ideal writer would evolve spontaneously. One in whom the powers of expression fully responded to the state of feeling, would unconsciously use that variety in the mode of presenting his thoughts, which Art demands. This constant employment of one species of phraseology, which all have now to strive against, implies an undeveloped faculty of language. To have a specific style is to be poor in speech. If we remember that, in the far past, men had only nouns and verbs to convey their ideas with, and that from then to now the growth has been towards a greater number of implements of thought, and consequently towards a greater complexity and variety in their combinations; we may infer that we are now, in our use of sentences, much what the primitive man was in his use of words; and that a continuance of the process that has hitherto gone on, must produce increasing heterogeneity in our modes of expression. As now, in a fine nature, the play of the features, the tones of the voice and its cadences, vary in harmony with every thought uttered; so, in one

possessed of a fully-developed power of speech, the mould
in which each combination of words is cast will similarly
vary with, and be appropriate to the sentiment.

68. That a perfectly-endowed man must unconsciously
write in all styles, we may infer from considering how
styles originate. Why is Johnson pompous, Goldsmith
simple? Why is one author abrupt, another rhythmical,
another concise? Evidently in each case the habitual mode
of utterance must depend upon the habitual balance of the
nature. The predominant feelings have by use trained the
intellect to represent them. But while long, though unconscious, discipline has made it do this efficiently, it remains from lack of practice, incapable of doing the same for
the less active feelings; and when these are excited, the
usual verbal forms undergo but slight modifications. Let
the powers of speech be fully developed, however — let the
ability of the intellect to utter the emotions be complete; and
this fixity of style will disappear. The perfect writer will
express himself as Junius, when in the Junius frame of
mind; when he feels as Lamb felt, will use a like familiar
speech; and will fall into the ruggedness of Carlyle when
in a Carlylean mood. Now he will be rhythmical and now
irregular; here his language will be plain and there ornate;
sometimes his sentences will be balanced and at other times
unsymmetrical; for a while there will be considerable same-
ness, and then again great variety. His mode of expression
naturally responding to his state of feeling, there will flow
from his pen a composition changing to the same degree
that the aspects of his subject change. He will thus without effort conform to what we have seen to be the laws of
effect. And while his work presents to the reader that
variety needful to prevent continuous exertion of the same
faculties, it will also answer to the description of all highly-
organized products, both of man and of nature: it will be
not a series of like parts simply placed in juxtaposition, but

one whole made up of unlike parts that are mutually dependent.[1]

[1] This is the fundamental principle with which, in the opinion of the editor, Mr. Spencer would have done well to open his essay. He would thus have brought his various exceptions, opposing rules, supplementary principles, and so forth, under one universal all-pervading law.

STYLE.

By T. H. Wright.

i. *Résumé of Spencer's Essay.*

1. A recent historian of Rome, towards the close of his famous attempt to undeceive the world at large with respect to the genius of Cicero, sums up his argument in the following words: — "Ciceronianism is a problem which, in fact, cannot be properly solved, but can only be resolved into that greater mystery of human nature — language, and the effect of language on the mind." [1]

2. These words are suggestive — suggestive, too, of a wider question than at first sight appears. That men are influenced by language at least as much as by ideas; that power of expression is intimately associated with mental grasp generally; even that a fascination is exercised by style to which nothing equivalent is found in the accompanying thought — these are acknowledged truths, readily granted. But it is a most singular thing that they are so readily granted: it is singular that the question is not oftener asked — Why is this so?

3. How is it that language, which is but the vehicle of thought, comes to have a force which is not the mere weight of that which it carries? Even where this is not the case, where there is an equivalence of value in both style and ideas, great conceptions being nobly expressed, how is it that the matter and the form seem to have independent claims upon the attention? In a word, what is

[1] Mommsen, History of Rome, Book V., Chap. 12.

that in language which is not mere *expressiveness* of the obvious intentions of the writer, but is yet a merit?

4. At first sight there appears to be a simple answer to the question. Any of the numerous treatises on style or rhetoric abound with rules for the embellishment of discourse: the reader learns the importance of a choice of fitting words, of the judicious use of figures of speech, of the effect of melodious sentences and suitable cadences: he is instructed in the manipulation of complex constructions, and discovers the force of the gradation, the antithesis, and the climax: in short, he is easily led to the conclusion that, besides *expressiveness*, language may have the merit of *beauty*.

5. That this distinction is a superficial one has been shown with great ability in an article by Mr. Herbert Spencer on the 'Philosophy of Style.' He there traces all excellence of composition to two principles — Economy of the Attention, and Economy of the Sensibility of the recipient. Assuming that a reader can have at his command only a definite amount of power of attention, it is clear that whatever part of this is employed on the form of a composition must be subtracted, and leave so much the less to be occupied in the matter. In its popular aspect this is a truth familiar to all. If any author is said to have an obscure style, it is meant that his form obstructs his matter — that it absorbs an inordinate amount of the reader's attention. If he is tedious, it is because his language, by its monotony or redundancy, exhausts our energies, and leaves us correspondingly deficient in the mental vigour to be devoted to what he has to say.

6. But Mr. Spencer pushes his theory yet further. He shows, with great ingenuity, how various ornaments of style, at first sight most remote from mere utility, are in reality but devices of language which subserve the same purpose of economizing attention. Thus the canon which

prefers words of Saxon to words of Latin origin is justified by the greater familiarity of the former, recalling the associations of childhood, and their comparative brevity, which adds to their force what it diminishes from the effort required to recognize them. On the other hand, the occasional effect of polysyllabic words is attributed to their associated significance: for the effort involved in deciphering or using them, by hinting at a corresponding weightiness in the things implied, gives a force to an epithet which may do for a sentence. The same principle which explains the rules for choice of words is also found adequate to the solution of the reasons why some one order of words is more effective than another; why certain sequences of sentences are better than others; what are the respective merits of the direct and indirect style; and so forth. Then follows an analysis of the various figures of speech — Metaphor, Simile, and the like — in which their amenableness to the same law is established: and, finally, the applicability of the theory, even to the complex imagery of the poet, is exhibited in a passage which it would be an injustice to the writer not to quote at length :

7. "Passing on to a more complex application of the doctrine with which we set out, it must now be remarked that not only in the structure of sentences, and the use of figures of speech, may economy of the recipient's mental energy be assigned as the cause of force ; but that in the choice and arrangement of the minor images, out of which some large thought is to be built up, we may trace the same condition to effect. To select from the sentiment, scene, or event described, those typical elements which carry many others along with them ; and so, by saying a few things, but suggesting many, to- abridge the description ; is the secret of producing a vivid impression. An extract from Tennyson's 'Mariana' will well illustrate this :

> " ' All day within the dreamy house
> The door upon the hinges creaked,
> The blue-fly sung i' the pane, the mouse
> Behind the mouldering wainscot shrieked,
> Or from the crevice peered about.'

The several circumstances here specified bring with them many appropriate associations. Our attention is rarely drawn by the buzzing of a fly in the window, save when everything is still. While the inmates are moving about the house, mice usually keep silence; and it is only when extreme quietness reigns that they peep from their retreats. Hence each of the facts mentioned, presupposing numerous others, calls up these with more or less distinctness; and revives the feeling of dull solitude with which they are connected in our experience. Were all these facts detailed, instead of suggested, the attention would be so frittered away that little impression of dreariness would be produced. Similarly in other cases. Whatever the nature of the thought to be conveyed, this skilful selection of a few particulars which imply the rest is the key to success. In the choice of competent ideas, as in the choice of expressions, the aim must be to convey the greatest quantity of thoughts with the smallest quantity of words."

8. But Mr. Spencer does not rest content with deducing what may be called the adventitious charms of poetry from this principle; he even thinks that its distinctive characteristic — the restrictions of metre — may be explained by the same law. "The pleasure," he says, "which its measured movement gives us is ascribable to the comparative ease with which words metrically arranged can be recognized." Most people will be startled at the first sight of this bold dictum, but Mr. Spencer is not the man to shrink from the logical consequences of his principles, and they lead to more than this.

9. Any one who has attentively read the article, or even

the brief *résumé* of it just given, will have seen that the theory furnishes a canon for determining, with some degree of certainty, which of two styles is the better. To quote again: —"The relative goodness of any two modes of express-ing an idea may be determined by observing which requires the shortest process of thought for its comprehension."

10. Clearly, then, there must, in every case, be some form of expression which is absolutely the best; in other words, there is such a thing as an ideal style. Mr. Spencer accepts the conclusion, but at the same time reminds us that style must vary with its subject-matter.

11. "The perfect writer will express himself as Junius, when in the Junius frame of mind; when he feels as Lamb felt, will use a like familiar speech; and will fall into the ruggedness of Carlyle when in a Carlylean mood."

12. The reservation is a proper one, and with it the argument seems unimpeachable. Yet when Mr. Spencer throws the conclusion into the form of an epigram, and tells us that "to have a specific style is to be poor in speech," he makes the utmost possible demand upon our loyalty to exact reasoning. Like Adeimantus in the ' Republic,' we are "confounded by this novel kind of draughts-playing, played with words for counters."

ii. *Style the Imperfect Expression of the Writer's Personality.*

13. But if the foregoing theory be carefully reviewed, it will be seen that throughout it the treatment is what may be described as objective rather than subjective. Or, to avoid words in which there is a degree of ambiguity, the definite product language is more or less isolated from the agency using it, and viewed more in relation to the reader's than the writer's mind.[1] But there is another aspect of

---

[1] The last two paragraphs of Spencer's essay deal with the subjective aspect of the theory.

the relation, which cannot be left out without producing a
result which must be onesided and may be inaccurate. The
following pages will be an attempt to supply this omission
by a consideration of the nature of the various devices of
language, regarded as the outcome of the mind that employs
them.

14. That " to have a specific style is to be poor in speech "
has not been implied in the judgments which the world has
from time to time passed upon its greatest writers. Perhaps it would be nearer the truth to say that much in proportion as an author has reached a high eminence in his art
there has been found in his productions a corresponding tendency to an individuality of expression. Is it not a common complaint against inferior artists, whether in prose or
verse, in painting or music, that their compositions lack
character and originality? Uniformity is the distinguishing feature of mediocrity, while the work of genius is at
once recognized and attributed to the origin whose impress
it bears. And a little reflection will show that this is
exactly what is meant by "style." Various tricks of voice,
gesture, and dress are associated by every one with his
friends, glimpses of the hidden self being granted in such
half-unnoticed revelations. The chief value, indeed, of such
peculiarities rests in the fact that they are commonly un-
known to the man himself. For all of us, even the most
sincere, are to a certain extent actors in our intercourse
with others, and play a part that has been self-assigned,
often without due pondering of the player's power. Nature,
however, peeps out in countless little traits of character,
which find their expression in language, habit, and even in
movements. By what subtle union such tricks of manner
are linked with what Dr. Johnson has called " the anfrac-
tuosities of the human mind " is a curious and intricate
question, but no one will doubt the fact of the connection.
" That's father! " cries the child as she hears the well-

known footfall in the hall; "How like the man!" we ex-
claim when some characteristic remark is reported to us.[1]
Spite of the progress in complexity from a sound to a sentiment, each obeys the same law; and the connection between the footfall and the foot, between the speech and the
mind that conceived it, is one and the same.

15. Let us follow out the thought a little further. Not
only, to put the fact in its popular aspect, has every one
his peculiarities; but there are degrees of peculiarity accompanying degrees of individuality; as a man deviates in
character from the type ordinarily met with, so are his
habits singular to himself, till a point is reached where the
personality is remarkable, and the behaviour eccentric.
Where such manners are perfectly unaffected they are a
reflection of a self that stands alone among many, so that
the common dictum, that genius is eccentric, has a philosophical foundation.[2] There is no need to linger on the
numerous and tolerably obvious reservations which make
it impossible to convert the proposition, in other words, to
infer unusual power from singularity; the broad fact remains that where there is that marked originality called
genius, it is an originality not of thought, emotion, or pur-
suits, but of the man.

16. The application of this to literary style is easy, and
will be found to lead to some interesting results.

17. In its powers of direct expression, language is tolerably efficient, and were there nothing but facts, considered

---

[1] See the remarks of Theodore Watts (Encycl. Brit. 9th ed., Vol. 19,
p. 265) on the word 'wrought,' which Shakespeare puts into Othello's
mouth.

[2] "A muddle-headed person is a genius spoiled in the making. I think
it will be admitted that all *eminently* muddle-headed persons have the
temperament of genius. They are constantly breaking away from the
usual consecutions of concretes. A common associator by contiguity is too
closely tied to routine to get muddle-headed." — James, 'Psychology,' II.,
p. 352.

objectively, to be conveyed, even a simpler vehicle would
suffice. Swift, in one of the most humorous passages of
'Gulliver's Travels' describes a set of philosophers, who, dis-
daining language as the ordinary means of expressing their
thoughts, preferred to carry with them a pack of the things
most commonly referred to in every day parlance, by the
dexterous manipulation of which they contrived to carry on
long conversations. Now this represents, with the necessary
freedom of caricature, a real truth with regard to a certain
class of discourse. In any written composition, the less
the author's personality is involved in the matter treated
the simpler the language which suffices. The extreme form
of this truth is found in the case of algebra, where the
discourse is, so to speak, perfectly dispassionate, and the
symbolism perfectly adequate. Similarly, the language employed in mathematical proof is found adequate in proportion as the statements are purely objective. As we ascend
in the scale of literary composition the author's personality
creeps in, and brings with it a corresponding complexity of
language, not merely the complexity of structure of sentences, but of choice of words, use of figures of speech, and
all the refinements of elaborate writing. It is true that much
more than this has to be taken into consideration; the subjects themselves are infinitely more complex as the scale is
ascended, the distinctions are more delicate, the contrasts
present more sides to view, the gradations are subtler. But
is not this a corollary from the main principle? Is it not
because we are then dealing either with facts of our own or
the general consciousness; with ideas, emotions, desires, and
so forth; or at any rate with external facts looked at from
the point of view of an interested and questioning observer,
that there is this increase in complexity, or, in other words,
decrease in adequacy of language?

18. But this idea admits of yet further development. The
facts perfectly expressed in algebraical symbols receive a

nearly perfect expression in mathematical language. The terminology of science is found very tolerably sufficient, if strictly adhered to, and mostly where expository and descriptive. In history and biography what we may call the subjective element is strong, and there we find all the refinements of composition. These express, not only facts and aspects of facts, not only are there delicate implications of expression, embodied in all the recognized figures of rhetoric, the trope, the simile, and the metaphor; but there are the glimpses at the very self of the author which lurks in unconscious tricks of diction and turns of thought, and emerges in epithets, in repetitions, and in phrases. In poetry the author reigns supreme, and there too the imperfection of language is most manifest. In a very fine passage every word is charged with meaning and riveted to its place, in fact the vehicle is strained to its utmost to bear the load imposed upon it. Hence Coleridge's well-known definition [1] of poetry as "the best words in the best order." Meanwhile the personality of the Poet pervades every line of every poem, a hardly recognized but unfailing presence. He colours each picture, and is a spectator at every scene; he is beside Ulysses in the island of Calypso; with him he witnesses the death of Argus and the insolence of the suitors; he shares the recognition of Penelope and the welcome to home; and when dire retribution seizes the usurpers he looks upon their fall.

19. Not that this personality is directly obtruded upon the hearer's notice; in the instance of Homer, it is markedly withdrawn, the characters speak of themselves, the descriptions are meant to serve no moral end. But what is never brought before us as an avowed element in the composition is everywhere present in the form of the narrative, — we

---

[1] 'Table Talk,' July 12, 1827. "I wish our clever young poets would remember my homely definitions of prose and poetry; that is, prose = words in their best order; poetry = the *best* words in the best order."

never hear the accents of the voice, though we are always
listening to its tones. Take as an illustration of this a
passage of pure description from the 'Odyssey'[1]:—

πῦρ μὲν ἐπ' ἐσχαρόφιν μέγα καίετο, τηλόθι δ' ὀδμὴ
κέδρου τ' εὐκεάτοιο θύου τ' ἀνὰ νῆσον ὀδώδει
δαιομένων· ἡ δ' ἔνδον ἀοιδιάουσ' ὀπὶ καλῇ,
ἱστὸν ἐποιχομένη χρυσείῃ κερκίδ' ὕφαινεν.
ὕλη δὲ σπέος ἀμφὶ πεφύκει τηλεθόωσα,
κλήθρη τ' αἴγειρός τε καὶ εὐώδης κυπάρισσος.
ἔνθα δέ τ' ὄρνιθες τανυσίπτεροι εὐνάζοντο,
σκῶπές τ' ἴρηκές τε τανύγλωσσοί τε κορῶναι
εἰνάλιαι, τῇσίν τε θαλάσσια ἔργα μέμηλεν.
ἡ δ' αὐτοῦ τετάνυστο περὶ σπείους γλαφυροῖο
ἡμερὶς ἡβώωσα, τεθήλει δὲ σταφυλῇσι·
κρῆναι δ' ἑξείης πίσυρες ῥέον ὕδατι λευκῷ,
πλησίαι ἀλλήλων τετραμμέναι ἄλλυδις ἄλλη.
ἀμφὶ δὲ λειμῶνες μαλακοὶ ἴου ἠδὲ σελίνου
θήλεον· ἔνθα κ' ἔπειτα καὶ ἀθάνατός περ ἐπελθὼν
θηήσαιτο ἰδὼν καὶ τερφθείη φρεσὶν ᾗσιν.

Odyssey, V. 59-74.

1 "And on the hearth there was a great fire burning, and from afar was
smelt the fragrance of cleft cedar and of sandal wood, blazing through the
isle. And the nymph within was singing with a sweet voice as she fared
to and fro before the loom and wove with a shuttle of gold. And round
about the cave there was a wood blossoming, alder and poplar and sweet-
smelling cypress. And therein all birds, long of wing, had their places of
rest, owls and falcons and chattering sea-crows, which have their business
in the waters. And lo! there about the hollow cave trailed a gadding gar-
den vine, all rich with clusters. And the wells of four streams set orderly
were running with clear water, hard by one another, turned each to a separate course. Moreover, all around soft meadows of violets and parsley
blossomed, yea, even a deathless god who came there might wonder at the
sight and be glad at heart." —Butcher and Lang's Translation.

20. An analysis of this passage which points out its beauties will be found also to draw attention precisely to those parts where the author's presence is latent. The smell of the cedar and the voice of the divine songstress accompanying the music of her loom, are, by the epithets "fragrant" and "sweet" made part of the real or imagined experience of the poet; while the word ἐποιχομένη suggests, and just suggests, glimpses that he catches of her form as she moves at her work within the cave. Then he describes the wood that shades her abode, implying, by an epithet, how that too appeals to another sense, joining with the incense that burns close by in a mixture of pleasant smells. Another feature is introduced: there are birds harbouring in the branches, and the word εὐνάζοντο that describes this, by an implied comparison with the sleeping-chambers of man, shows a sort of tender way of looking at nature. It is more than if it were merely said, "there were birds in the branches." Again, the allusion to the sea in the words τῆσίν τε θαλάσσια ἔργα μέμηλεν is a direct reflection of the poet's, in no way forming part of a description merely meant to call up an actual scene, instead of a particular way of looking at a scene. The same is true of the words that describe the vine, bending with its burden of ripe clusters, of the labyrinth of streams, and the patches of violet and parsley round them: the accompanying adjectives draw attention to beauties the poet has noticed, and wishes us to notice as well. There is hardly need to point out how the words with which the whole concludes are but an exclamation of wonder and admiration on the part of the poet at the scene he has called up.

21. But this is not all, for besides the selection of these various elements there is the mode of their combination into a definite picture, the order in which the images follow one another, and the gradation and transition of ideas which are all part of the art, that is, of the mind — of the *self* of the

author. At a distance the senses of sight and smell are first caught by the glimmer of the fire and the fragrance of what is burning in it; as Hermes approaches he hears the sound of the goddess singing at her work; coming still closer, he has leisure to mark the minute details of the scene, the cavern, the grove, and the vine; while the words ἀθάνατός περ in the concluding lines leave him in amazement at the beauty of the whole.

22. Now this may sound like hypercriticism, and it would be hypercriticism if it were meant that all these points were before the mind of the poet, forming part of an intentional study of effect. On the contrary, the implication is the direct reverse. It is because Homer was such or such a man, because he had been in the habit of regarding what he saw after a certain fashion of his own, that when he set himself to compose poetry he composed it as he did. Hence there is a deep meaning in the saying of Milton,[1] that he who would write good poetry must make his life a poem. It is by virtue of a thousand minute traits of character, the gradual deposit of life's experiences, that any one speaks, writes, even walks and moves, as we see him do. For there must be some reason why, if two men set about describing a scene, or giving even a plain, unvarnished account of some event, the mode of their narration differs, differs, too, in such a way that each can be ascribed to its author, as we say, by internal evidence, that is, by its style. While, then, no better explanation appears, that theory of style may perhaps be provisionally accepted which identifies it with character — with unconscious revelations of the hidden self.

23. This conclusion needs a little further elaboration before it is compared with that view of what is called the

---

[1] " He who would not be frustrate of his hope to write well hereafter in laudable things, ought himself to be a true poem, that is, a composition and pattern of the best and honorablest things." — ' Apology against a Pamphlet called A Modest Confutation, etc.'

philosophy of style, which resolves all the devices of composition into schemes for economizing the reader's attention. It is necessary to point out, and this may be done briefly, how not only is style generally the impress of the author's self, but that there is a correspondence between the distinctive features of any particular passage and the points at which, in the manner just indicated, the writer's personality glides into the discourse. This is not difficult, if what has been already said be accepted. What indeed is meant by saying that an author is best where his writing is most natural ?

24. Is it not implied that the happiest touches are those which are original — that those phrases and expressions are most welcome to the reader which set the matter they convey in a new light — and that the light in which the writer himself sees it ? If the foregoing passage from the 'Odyssey' be reviewed it will be found that its beauties are coincident with the parts where the presence of the poet seems to be hinted, and this is equally true, though not equally discernible, in all writing that is at all elaborate.

25. Now, how does all this square with the dictum that "to have a specific style is to be poor in speech"? It will not at first sight appear so very incompatible. In a certain sense, style at all owes its existence to the imperfection of the vehicle of thought. Were language a perfectly adequate means of embodying ideas, what is now to be looked for in the *mode* of statement would be found directly declared in the statement itself. For the countless devices of language, the gestures and tones of discourse, the thousand rhetorical figures of written composition, are really one and all simple propositions not capable of exact expression in the body of the narrative. They are the lights and shades of the picture, or perhaps rather the finer touches, which are to tickle the imagination of the reader with suggested beauties. And it is exactly in these refinements of expression that the deepest

meaning of any author, in other words, his *self* resides. There is something pathetic in the reflection that we walk this world half hidden from one another, a constant struggle going on to make known the thoughts, beliefs, and aspirations of the real but partly imprisoned being, which never can be known exactly as they are to any but the mind that conceives them.[1] Like savages, we speak mostly by signs, which serve us well enough, but leave much uncommunicated. It is well, however, that this imperfection is an imperfection that produces beauty, that the grating of the machine is not harsh, but musical. Mr. Herbert Spencer is successful in showing that the various devices of language do serve to the economy of the reader's attention, and that beauties of style are beauties partly because they effect this end. But he has not raised a question which seems closely akin to the subject. Why is it needful to have recourse to these expedients at all, and why is there an infinite variety in every man's use of them? The answer to these questions seems to give an insight into a higher law, to which Mr. Spencer's principle stands rather as an empirical generalization. It is this: — that each man's inmost nature is a secret to all but himself — and that a secret which in no two cases is the same. Every

[1] " The clearness and tact demanded by the French, which I am bound to confess, compel one to say only part of what one thinks and are damaging to depth of thought, seemed to me so much tyranny. The French care to express only that which is clear. As it happens, the most important truths, those relating to the transformations of life, are not clear; one perceives them only in a kind of half-light. That is why, after having been the first to perceive the truth of what is called Darwinism nowadays, France has been the last to rally to it. They saw it well enough, but it was out of the beaten track of the language, it did not fit the mould of well-constructed phrases. In that way France passed by the side of precious truths, not without seeing them, but simply flinging them among the waste paper as useless or impossible to express. At the start I wanted to say everything, and I often said it badly. At the risk of tumbling into the realm of the unintelligible, I endeavored to fix the fleeting essence, hitherto considered as not worthy of consideration." —Renan, 'The Future of Science,' Preface.

attempt to communicate it partly fails, and so language is full of compromises and expedients; each nature to be revealed is different, and so there is a countless variety of styles. This then is not due to poverty of speech, rather it is due to multiplicity of individualities, each speaking its own language and telling its own tale.

26. The ideal style, then, is but for an ideal being who is to be without personality. The perfect writer may write, now like Junius, now like Lamb, now like Carlyle, but like himself he can never write. He cannot, as we say, express *himself.* A significant phrase, for after all it is when a man, as far as he can, expresses *himself,* that his communication is most worth having. It is the one thing of which he certainly knows something, where he can indeed speak with authority. It is not so much what a man knows, as how he knows it, not so much the extent as the quality of his information, that gains him a right to be heard. Originality is far oftener originality of expression than idea, a fresh aspect of something old, not a discovery of something new. And so there starts up here an answer to the difficulties encountered at the outset, " Why men are influenced by language at least as much as by ideas " : and " Why power of expression is intimately associated with mental grasp generally." Partly, no doubt, because in language resides the personality of the speaker or writer, and men are influenced by personality — but far more for another reason. The highest form of ability is something which pervades the whole being ; it is not restricted to an intellect preternaturally acute, to vividness of imagination, or fineness of feeling ; but it is the manifestation of a nature — of a *self,* which is really great. And it has been seen that it is in expression, or style, that the self of the author is to be sought. That, then, is a true instinct which so intimately associates power of expression with power of character generally. Of this power, too, the distinguishing

feature is its individuality. Just as in animal life the ascent of the scale of creation is a process of differentiation of functions; just as a higher form of life is marked off from a lower form by greater speciality of shape, by powers more accurately defined, by habits more peculiarly its own; so in the comparison of man with man, something similar to this law is traceable, pointing out that the superiority of genius in degree is mainly a consequence of its difference in kind.

27. Thus nature seems to speak in a continued protest against uniformity, by a thousand analogies insisting upon the supreme importance of the individual. And the critical verdict which pronounces that writing best which is the most natural can be affiliated to as wide a law as this. Whether or no it be thought that each man is put into the world the possessor of some particular truth, which his acts or words can set before his fellow-creatures, it is at any rate clear that the inevitable specialty of each man's experiences must present things to him in an aspect which can be exactly the same for no other. There are no real *doubles* in the world, no such thing as identity in constitution and circumstances. While, then, this is so, there is a significance in style, a value in the unconscious self-revelations of traits of personality. However a man may fail of the object he sets before him in what he does or says, yet if there has been in him that conscientious fidelity to his purpose, which is but an attempt to express *himself*, his work will not have been wasted, though its direct worth be unimportant.

APPENDIX A.

THE SOUND-ELEMENT IN VERSE.

" This gratification (*i.e.* that produced by the mere sound of verse) such as it is, is of an entirely positive kind, acting directly on the sense.   It would not have occurred to me that there could be a doubt about this, had not Mr. Spencer, in his essay on the ' Philosophy of Style,' taken another view. He ingeniously refers forcible style to economy of the reader's or hearer's attention, and makes out his point very successfully in many particulars ; but he seems to me quite to fail in his attempt to bring the effect of rhythmical structure in verse under the same rule.   He says, ' If, as we have seen, there is an expenditure of mental energy in the mere act of listening to verbal articulations, or in that silent repetition of them which goes on in reading — if the perceptive faculties must be in active exercise to identify every syllable — then any mode of so combining words as to present a regular recurrence of certain traits which the mind can anticipate, will diminish that strain upon the attention required by the total irregularity of prose.   Just as the body, in receiving a series of varying concussions, must keep the muscles ready to meet the most violent of them, as not knowing when such may come ; so the mind, in receiving unarranged articulations, must keep its perceptives active enough to recognize the least easily caught sounds.   And as, if the concussions occur in a definite order, the body may husband its forces by adjusting the resistance needful for each concussion ; so, if the syllables be rhythmically arranged, the mind may economize its energies by anticipating the attention required for each syllable.'

"There is surely a confusion here between the intellect
and the ear, and between two distinct meanings of perception,
namely, the *recognition* of a syllable as a known word or
part of a known word, and the mere *hearing* of it as part of
a series of accented and unaccented sounds. The 'least
easily caught sounds' are those which, from softness or
indistinctness, it is *hardest to recognize* as known words
or parts of known words; but these are no less easily and
completely *heard* as belonging to the regular series of
alternating sounds than the louder accented constituents
of the series. As regards the mere act of *hearing*, the
perception of the series is an affection which would be as
easily produced by nonsense-syllables arranged in the same
rhythm : and as for attention, not *less* but *more* of it would
seem to be involved in the case of a regular accented series
than in prose. For against the supposition that the ear is
relieved at alternate instants from the strain of its expectant
attitude, through foreknowledge of the place of the louder
syllables, we must set the fact that in verse it is actively on
the watch, and notices with positive satisfaction the rhythmical succession *as such;* while in an irregular series it is
not the least on the watch for the purely *sound*-qualities of
what is going on, but acts as the uninterested and passive
conductor of symbols to the mind. The intellectual *recognition* of the sounds, on the other hand, as known words or
parts of known words, is in no way facilitated by their
rhythmical succession. There are as many comparatively
loud and distinct syllables, and as many comparatively
faint and indistinct ones, in a paragraph of prose as in
an equally long paragraph of verse : and the sum of mental energy required to identify them is equal in the two
cases. The fact that in the verse the *ear* is aware before-
hand at what instant the louder and fainter syllables are
coming cannot relieve the *intellect* of its labour of recognition; for difficulty or ease of recognition is simply a func-

tion of the distinctness with which the syllable is heard when it comes, and of nothing else.

"Mr. Spencer's analogy of muscular adjustment is misleading. For in a succession of *precisely similar* bodily impulses, we are aware of exactly what is coming, and so can prepare for it before it comes : but in the case of a mental effort, we have no idea what it is to be till the matter of it is presented ; and the recognition of every syllable is a *different* act from the recognition of every other, and entails different tracts of association. The fairer analogue would be a portrait, which we certainly should not recognize any the more easily for knowing that such an effort would be demanded of us at some particular moment. In the case of purely physical stimulation, there is a preparation of a certain amount of nervous energy against a particular instant when the repetition of the stimulus leads to its discharge ; and if the stimulus does not come at that instant, the closing of the expected outlet for the discharge gives us annoyance. But an act of recognition is a mental process which begins naturally at any moment on the presentation of the symbol to be recognized : and whatever its objective nervous counterpart may be, it certainly cannot be amenable to regular rhythmic discharge." — GURNEY, 'Power of Sound,' p. 441, note.

"It must be remembered that the beauty of sound in poetry is to a great extent indirect, being supplied by the passion or emotion which the ideas symbolized by the sounds arouse. The beauty of poetical sound in itself is very likely less than often supposed. It must have the capacity for receiving passionate expression ; but that is not the same as the sensuous beauty of a note or a colour. If the words used in a noble poem were divested of all meaning, they would lose much, though not all, of the beauty of their sound." — B. BOSANQUET, note in his translation of Hegel's 'Introduction to Philosophy of Fine Art,' p. 172.

APPENDIX B.

THE EVOLUTION OF LITERATURE.

"THE lowest form of language is the exclamation, by
which an entire idea is vaguely conveyed through a single
sound; as among the lower animals. That human language
ever consisted solely of exclamations, and so was strictly
homogeneous in respect of its parts of speech, we have no
evidence. But that language can be traced down to a form
in which nouns and verbs are its only elements, is an established fact. In the gradual multiplication of parts of speech
out of these primary ones — in the differentiation of verbs
into active and passive, of nouns into abstract and concrete
— in the rise of distinctions of mood, tense, person, of number and case — in the formation of auxiliary verbs, of adjectives, adverbs, pronouns, prepositions, articles — in the
divergence of those orders, genera, species, and varieties of
parts of speech by which civilized races express minute
modifications of meaning — we see a change from the homogeneous to the heterogeneous. And it may be remarked,
in passing, that it is more especially in virtue of having
carried this subdivision of functions to a greater extent and
completeness, that the English language is superior to all
others. Another aspect under which we may trace the
development of language, is the differentiation of words of
allied meanings. Philology early disclosed the truth that
in all languages words may be grouped into families having
a common ancestry. An aboriginal name, applied indiscriminately to each of an extensive and ill-defined class of
things or actions, presently undergoes modifications by

64

which the chief divisions of the class are expressed. These several names springing from the primitive root, themselves become the parents of other names still further modified. And by the aid of those systematic modes which presently arise, of making derivatives and forming compound terms expressing still smaller distinctions, there is finally developed a tribe of words so heterogeneous in sound and meaning, that to the uninitiated it seems incredible they should have had a common origin. Meanwhile, from other roots there are being evolved other such tribes, until there results a language of some sixty thousand or more unlike words, signifying as many unlike objects, qualities, acts. Yet another way in which language in general advances from the homogeneous to the heterogeneous, is in the multiplication of languages. Whether, as Max Müller and Bunsen think, all languages have grown from one stock, or whether, as some philologists say, they have grown from two or more stocks, it is clear that since large families of languages, as the Indo-European, are of one parentage, they have become distinct through a process of continuous divergence. The same diffusion over the earth's surface which has led to the differentiation of the race, has simultaneously led to a differentiation of their speech: a truth which we see further illustrated in each nation by the peculiarities of dialect found in separate districts. Thus the progress of language conforms to the general law, alike in the evolution of languages, in the evolution of families of words, and in the evolution of parts of speech.

"On passing from spoken to written language, we come upon several classes of facts, all having similar implications. Written language is connate with Painting and Sculpture ; and at first all three are appendages of Architecture, and have a direct connection with the primary form of all government — the theocratic. Merely noting by the way the fact that sundry wild races, as for example the Austra-

lians and the tribes of South Africa, are given to depicting
personages and events upon the walls of caves, which are
probably regarded as sacred places, let us pass to the case
of the Egyptians. Among them, as also among the Assyr-
ians, we find mural paintings used to decorate the temple
of the god and the palace of the king (which were, indeed,
originally identical) ; and as such they were governmental
appliances in the same sense that state-pageants and religious feasts were. Further, they were governmental appliances in virtue of representing the worship of the god, the
triumphs of the god-king, the submission of his subjects,
and the punishment of the rebellious. And yet again they
were governmental, as being the products of an art rever-
enced by the people as a sacred mystery. From the
habitual use of this pictorial representation, there naturally
grew up the but slightly-modified practice of picture-writing
—a practice which was found still extant among the Mexicans at the time they were discovered. By abbreviations
analogous to those still going on in our own written and
spoken language, the most familiar of these pictured figures
were successively simplified; and ultimately there grew up
a system of symbols, most of which had but a distant
resemblance to the things for which they stood. The
inference that the hieroglyphics of the Egyptians were
thus produced, is confirmed by the fact that the picture-
writing of the Mexicans was found to have given birth to a
like family of ideographic forms; and among them, as
among the Egyptians, these had been partially differentiated
into the kuriological or imitative, and the tropical or sym-
bolic : which were, however, used together in the same rec-
ord. In Egypt, written language underwent a further differentiation ; whence resulted the hieratic and the epistolo-
graphic or enchorial : both of which are derived from the
original hieroglyphic. At the same time we find that for
the expression of proper names, which could not be other-

wise conveyed, phonetic symbols were employed; and though it is alleged that the Egyptians never actually achieved complete alphabetic writing, yet it can scarcely be doubted that these phonetic symbols occasionally used in aid of their ideographic ones, were the germs out of which alphabetic writing grew. Once having become separate from hieroglyphics, alphabetic writing itself underwent numerous differentiations — multiplied alphabets were produced: between most of which, however, more or less connection can still be traced. And in each civilized nation there has now grown up for the representation of one set of sounds, several sets of written signs, used for distinct purposes. Finally, through a yet more important differentiation came printing; which, uniform in kind as it was at first, has since become multiform.

"While written language was passing through its earlier stages of development, the mural decoration which formed its root was being differentiated into painting and sculpture. The gods, kings, men, and animals represented, were originally marked by indented outlines and coloured. In most cases these outlines were of such depth, and the object they circumscribed so far rounded and marked out in its leading parts, as to form a species of work intermediate between intaglio and bas-relief. In other cases we see an advance upon this: the raised places between the figures being chiselled off, and the figures themselves appropriately tinted, a painted bas-relief was produced. The restored Assyrian architecture at Sydenham, exhibits this style of art carried to greater perfection — the persons and things represented, though still barbarously coloured, are carved out with more truth and in greater detail; and in the winged lions and bulls used for the angles of gateways, we may see a considerable advance towards a completely sculptured figure; which, nevertheless, is still coloured, and still forms part of the building. But while in Assyria the production of a statue proper, seems to have been little, if at all, attempted, we may trace in Egyptian art the gradual separation of the sculptured figure from the wall. A walk through the collection in the British Museum will clearly show this; while it will at the same time afford an opportunity of observing the evident traces which the independent statues bear of their derivation from bas-relief : seeing that nearly all of them not only display that union of the limbs with the body which is the characteristic of bas-relief, but have the back of the statue united from head to foot with a block which stands in place of the original wall. Greece repeated the leading stages of this progress. As in Egypt and Assyria, these twin arts were at first united with each other and with their parent, Architecture; and were the aids of religion and government. On the friezes of Greek temples, we see coloured bas-reliefs representing sacrifices, battles, processions, games — all in some sort religious. On the pediments we see painted sculptures more or less united with the tympanum, and having for subjects the triumphs of gods or heroes. Even when we come to statues that are definitely separated from the buildings to which they pertain, we still find them coloured; and only in the later periods of Greek civilization, does the differentiation of sculpture from painting appear to have become complete. In Christian art we may clearly trace a parallel re-genesis. All early paintings and sculptures throughout Europe, were religious in subject — represented Christs, crucifixions, virgins, holy families, apostles, saints. They formed integral parts of church architecture, and were among the means of exciting worship: as in Roman Catholic countries they still are. Moreover, the early sculptures of Christ on the cross, of virgins, of saints, were coloured ; and it needs but to call to mind the painted madonnas and crucifixes still abundant in continental churches and highways, to perceive the significant fact

that painting and sculpture continue in closest connection
with each other, where they continue in closest connection
with their parent. Even when Christian sculpture was
pretty clearly differentiated from painting, it was still religious and governmental in its subjects — was used for
tombs in churches and statues of kings; while, at the same
time, painting, where not purely ecclesiastical, was applied
to the decoration of palaces, and besides representing royal
personages, was almost wholly devoted to sacred legends.
Only in quite recent times have painting and sculpture become entirely secular arts. Only within these few centuries has painting been divided into historical, landscape,
marine, architectural, genre, animal, still-life, &c., and sculp-
·ture grown heterogeneous in respect of the variety of real and
ideal subjects with which it occupies itself.

"Strange as it seems then, we find it no less true, that
all forms of written language, of painting, and of sculpture,
have a common root in the politico-religious decorations of
ancient temples and palaces. Little resemblance as they now
have, the bust that stands on the console, the landscape
that hangs against the wall, and the copy of the *Times* lying
upon the table, are remotely akin; not only in nature, but
by extraction. The brazen face of the knocker which the
postman has just lifted, is related not only to the wood-
cuts of the *Illustrated London News* which he is delivering,
but to the characters of the *billet-doux* which accompanies
it. Between the painted window, the prayer-book on which
its light falls, and the adjacent monument, there is consan-
guinity. The effigies on our coins, the signs over shops,
the figures that fill every ledger, the coat of arms outside
the carriage-panel, and the placards inside the omnibus, are,
in common with dolls, blue-books and paper-hangings, lin-
eally descended from the rude sculpture-paintings in which
the Egyptians represented the triumphs and worship of their

god-kings. Perhaps no example can be given which more vividly illustrates the multiplicity and heterogeneity of the products that in course of time may arise by successive differentiations from a common stock." SPENCER, 'First Principles,' pp. 162–7.

INDEX.

[The figures refer to the pages of the text.]

71

ADVERTISEMENTS

—

www.ingramcontent.com/pod-product-compliance
Lightning Source LLC
Chambersburg PA
CBHW031441270326
41930CB00007B/826

* 9 7 8 3 3 3 7 0 7 9 2 3 9 *